METAPHYSICAL DIVINE WISDOM
on Manifesting Fearless Assertive Confidence

A Practical Motivational Guide to Spirituality
Series

KEVIN HUNTER

WARRIOR
OF LIGHT
PRESS

Warrior of Light Press
www.kevin-hunter.com

First Edition: July 2019
Printed in the United States of America

All rights reserved. Copyright © 2019
ISBN-13: 978-1733196222

3. Mind and Body. 2. Spirituality. 1. Title

DEDICATION

For you on your soul's spiritual journey.

METAPHYSICAL DIVINE WISDOM
BOOK SERIES

On Psychic Spirit Team Heaven Communication
On Soul Consciousness and Purpose
On Increasing Prayer with Faith for an Abundant Life
On Balancing the Mind, Body, and Soul
On Manifesting Fearless Assertive Confidence
On Universal, Physical, Spiritual and Soul Love

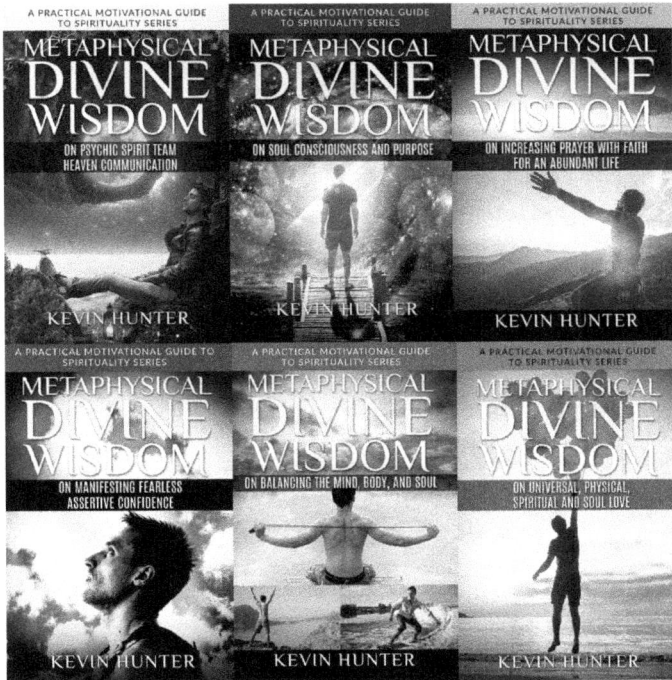

♥

Contents

»⬥«»⬥«»⬥«»⬥«»⬥«»⬥«»⬥«»

AUTHOR NOTE

The *Metaphysical Divine Wisdom* books are a series of spiritually based books that focus on different areas of ones life. Like many of my spiritual related metaphysical books, this one is also infused with practical messages and spirit guidance that my Spirit team has taught and shared with me revolving around many different topics. The main goal is to fine-tune your body, mind, and soul. Like all souls, you are a Divine communicator capable of receiving messages and guidance from Heaven.

My personal Spirit team council makes up God and the Holy Spirit, as well as a team of guides, angels, and sometimes Archangels and Saints. I am merely the liaison or messenger in delivering and interpreting the intentions of what they wish to communicate. My team comprises some hard truth telling Wise Ones from the other side, including Saint Nathaniel, who can be brutal in his direct forcefulness. He cuts right to the heart of humanity without apology. I have learned quite a bit from him while adopting his ideology, which is Heaven's philosophy as a whole. I wouldn't preach Divine Guidance that God doesn't whisper into my Clairaudient ear first.

If I use the word "He" when pertaining to God, this does not mean that I am advocating that he is a male. Simply replace the word, "He" with one you are comfortable using to identify God for you to be. If the word, "God" makes you uncomfortable, then substitute it with one you're more familiar with like Universe, Spirit, the Light, or any other comparable word. This goes for any gender I use as examples. When I say "spirit team", I am referring to a team of 'Guides and Angels'.

One of the purposes of my work is to empower, enlighten, as well as entertain. It's also to help you improve yourself, your soul, your life and humanity by default. If anything I am preaching to myself, because God knows that I can use a refresher course once in awhile. It does not matter if you are a beginner or well versed in the subject matter. There may be something that reminds you of something you already know or something that you were unaware of. We all have much to share with one another, as we are all one in the end.

~ Kevin Hunter

METAPHYSICAL DIVINE WISDOM
ON MANIFESTING FEARLESS ASSERTIVE CONFIDENCE

CHAPTER ONE

Combat Fear

I t's been noted that one's confidence can crumble upon losing things in the key practical areas of your life. You might feel a shattering of self-worth when you lose your job, a relationship, a friend, or your home. It's interesting to note how losing a material or physical possession affects your confidence and sense of self-worth. It can cause you to lose interest in activities in life that you once enjoyed. You may become bed ridden and depressed. You cancel plans, ignore phone calls and are unreachable for a period of time. In those instances that your confidence is shattered by a material or physical loss, then that's when your confidence is needed more than ever. The human ego has insisted upon you to base your confidence and self-worth on the things you've achieved and attained when the reverse is what should be the case. You've made physical material possessions an extension of yourself when all you need to rise up and thrive is already burning within you. It is the fearless assertive confidence you build and expand up within your soul first, then you use those traits to drive you towards attaining your desires.

The most successful people that came from a poor uneducated background and achieved their dreams did so based on the fearless assertive confidence they had within them first. They may not have had the degree or the money, but they did have a passionate Divine fire that filled them with confidence. This kind of fearless confidence doesn't cost any money, because it's a trait that your soul already owns.

When you lose any kind of physical or material possession, then that should be the drive that propels you to utilize the fearless confidence that is already burning within the pilot light of your soul. This part of your soul comes from the light you were made from where all things are possible.

When you lose anything of value that negatively affects your confidence, self-esteem and self-worth, then make that the driving force that propels you to rise up into warrior mode. Stand strong under that powerful Divine Light allowing it to be the nourishment your soul feeds off of that helps you move into manifesting a fearless assertive confidence. Fear is one of the most crippling and destructive energies that the Darkness infiltrates into anyone it can. Its goal is to witness your downfall by paralyzing you with fear.

Everyone experiences some form of fear at some point if not on a regular basis. Most anything fear based isn't real. It still doesn't stop you from conjuring up fear about what will or will not come. It's a matter of recognizing fear, looking it in the eye, and then running it over not allowing it to consume you. Fear is the opposite of faith. Fear starts with a false thought from the ego, and then the soul follows willingly believing it. It takes time and practice devoted to training oneself to ignore the fear and walk in faith.

Fear is one of the leading causes of soul and personal failure. It brings on paralysis, chaos, and procrastination. Moving past fear requires awareness of what you're attempting to defeat. Overcoming fear is no easy achievement. It can take a lifetime to conquer since the human soul has a built in ego that will do what it can to stop you from achievement. The ego is split into both the light and darkness of ego. The light ego being what gives you confidence to trust and believe in who you are and your abilities, while the darkness of ego twists that into greed, anger, or fear.

Every soul on the planet experiences fear throughout their Earthly life. It is the one common trait that everyone has listed in their soul contract before incarnating into an Earthly life. You're a feeling, breathing, thinking consciousness moving about in a physical vessel for a variety of reasons. Every single person on the planet has a reason for being here, even if you have no clue what it is at any given moment. It is up to you to discover your numerous purposes that are connected to one singular intention. There are the default motives that all are here such as learning to love, but there are other goals outside of that even though love is always at the top of the list in the end.

Where you are on the fear scale can range from the minimal to being consumed by a fear that drowns and paralyzes you. The more sensitive you are, then the more fear you are apt to brewing up inside. Use your sensitivities to your advantage and transmute any fear into self-confidence. Believe in yourself knowing that you are worthy if not more capable than any other to do what you are perpetually called to do.

One soul may be aware of internal fears and will ignore it by persevering anyway. Another soul will become crippled by fear and accomplish nothing in the process. The latter soul allows the grips of this invisible negative energy to plague their thoughts and entire being to the point of paralysis. The dreams they've always wanted to conquer never transpire due to this fear.

Fear breeds out of the ego, the part of you that gives you a sense of self-worth. When left unchecked the ego will run uncontrollably initiating all sorts of chaos and drama. The ego thrives on drama and negativity. This is what gives the beast life. Fear is manifested from the darkness of ego the same way a female gives birth to its child. Fear begins to grow and expand during your childhood development and upbringing. If you grew up in a household where you were constantly being told you're no good and will never amount to anything, then as you grow older and set out to accomplish your life purpose, the fears that rise up from conquering your purpose will incessantly talk you out of it. The ego will talk you out of accomplishing anything positive by filling your mind with thoughts you heard from others growing up through adolescence. The dark ego says, "You can't do that, you're not qualified, you are wasting your time, and you will never be a success at anything."

The repetitive words forever sift through your mind preventing you from taking action and getting to work. This creates a block that prevents you from going after what you desire. It is a block that forms a wall intended to disconnect you from the Divine. The Divine is where the answers, messages, and guidance reside in to help you travel down a smoother path while here.

The Dangers of Fear Energy

Avoid getting caught up in the grips of fear as you're channeling energy in a positive direction. Fear energy is one of the most dangerous energies ever attributed to humankind. For centuries it has been amazingly excessive triggering all sorts of destruction on the planet and on each other. From the perspective of an angel you can imagine what that looks like seeing comets darted around like a tennis ball getting everyone nowhere.

Fear and worry plague the planet to an unhealthy degree causing it to expand and shoot out into the universe only to dart right back down like a boomerang in an explosion. The fear and worry energy has been especially magnified due to how quickly information is transmitted through the media and Internet. This fear originates within all of the individual souls on Earth and multiplies creating a fire that burns and destroys everything in its wake. Fear and worry do nothing to help anyone.

Fear is one of the soul's worst enemies. It is the reason the planet is plagued with interpersonal and global battles. Fear is responsible for preventing you from achieving and conquering your purpose. Living in a space of fear is what blocks you from moving forward. Opportunities are lost due to fear because it ensures you remain paralyzed causing you to cower and hide from going after what you desire.

Fear stalls humanity from evolving as witnessed in the centuries of evolution on the planet. While progress continues to be made in diminutive trickles, improvement still moves at a glacial rate thanks to humanities fear. It should not take hundreds of years to advance in the tiniest steps despite taking what we can get. This is due to individual fear resisting against changing their perception and awakening their consciousness. Finding the space of love and respect is challenging for the mediocre mind. Training every breathing organism to snap out of it takes an army of lights to do their part. Extricate fear from your aura and become unstoppable.

I met a woman in her 60's who was a former

bank manager who quit and moved into semi-retirement. She wanted to supplement her income by becoming a Real Estate Agent on the side. The positive is she wouldn't have bank hours and could work when she chooses to on her own schedule. She walked into this new real estate career having zero experience not knowing the meaning of a counter offer. Six months after she started this new career she was closing $1 million plus homes in beach coastal cities. After one year, I started seeing her face on bus stop benches and freeway billboards.

Some people say they're too old for something or not qualified and have no experience, but this woman is a testament that she could do it IF she wanted it bad enough. She wanted it bad enough and went after it with joy, confidence, and passion, then conquered it in bigger ways than anyone imagined.

Fear is a ridiculously powerful dark energy that keeps you spinning around in the same spot ensuring you get nowhere. It causes you to hate others that are not like you or those that you don't understand. People that are unusual and dissimilar from the norm are more often than not the souls ushering in positive change in their individual way. They avoid following the herd and seem to be pushed to the forefront alone. That is one clue that you are standing in front of a soul leader.

Fear is controlled by what spiritual circles call the *ego* and religious circles call the *devil*. Either way both are interchangeable to describe the same thing, which is why I often vacillate between using both. The ego doesn't want to see you succeed and win. It wants to keep you feeling trapped and helpless. Work on releasing fears connected to anything in your life. Release it by handing it over to God, source, the universe, your higher self, the angels, your Spirit team, or whatever you're comfortable referring to it as.

You can say something like, "I don't want this, please take it. I'm not going to worry about this anymore. I'm going to let you do that while I focus on other things. And so it is."

Ignore the fear and run into the flames of possibilities knowing you may get burned, because at least you put yourself out there. You stood up for yourself by doing what you want to do. Your consciousness will be that much stronger, smarter, and powerful.

The attitude I've always had when diving into anything and everything I ever wanted fearlessly is to just dive on in. This means doing it anyway no matter what kind of fear energy attempts to get in the way. Nothing stops me when I'm operating from my highest self because I am worthy and qualified. That's not bad for someone that battles with social anxiety daily. You may be afraid of jumping, yet you still do it anyway because it's worth the risk to at least try to conquer your dreams. Reach that place where you can look back on your life and say, "I am a long way from where I've been."

In my life's trek to wellness from the brink of ruin with drug and alcohol addiction, I have risen up again and again. You are stronger than whatever is trying to tear you down. Recovery is sublime good hard work worth any price. Summon the nerve to get back up after any misfortune and don't let your life pass you by where it results in you getting the feeling that you've missed the boat. It is never too late to start anything you truly want to do. You are more powerful than you realize.

Fighting the Fear

Many human souls have passion and heart, but will do nothing with that Divine given gift out of fear. Fear is the #1 cause of turmoil in human souls. Fear comes from the ego and prevents you from going after your life purpose, your dream job, or the love interest. It is fear to speak your truth lovingly, or fear that stops you from going out and accomplishing things.

Some wrestle with anxiety due to their heightened sensitivities to the stimuli around them. Those with higher traits of anxiety, tend to be more in tune, psychic, or intuitive than other souls. They absorb more than the average person absorbs, and for that matter need to adopt a strict disciplined routine that is aligned with their personal equilibrium. Use your emotions to your advantage, since they house communication receptors with the Divine.

Anxiety rises when fear becomes too great, but most fears are outlandish, meaning that what you fear tends to be exaggerated. Notice what makes you fearful about something, then examine what that is to a high degree and note if the cause is more in your head rather than based in truth.

Sometimes it's not necessarily fear of failure, but fear of success that you're undeserving of rewards. You might feel guilty about it, but everyone deserves success and rewards. No soul is more special than another in the eyes of Heaven. Opportunities exist for you to take hold of and run with in the right spirit.

This is the same fear associated with the risk of pursuing a potential love interest. You might be afraid to approach your love crush for fear of being rejected, but if it's someone you can't get your mind off of, then take the risk to at least say hello to this person. Gauge their interest level after saying hello and notice if they seem standoffish because they're not interested or unfriendly due to shyness. Some people have given up a potential love interest intended for them out of fear, or they'll avoid approaching a potential partner out of fear. Fear is one of the greatest causes of human sabotage holding people back from achieving the life they desire. You don't want to wait until you're in the final days of life wishing you could go back into time and went after those things that were itching at you, but which you ignored and brushed aside out of procrastination, fear, or a lack of confident drive.

Many ignore the windows of opportunity revealed to them by spirit and wind up watching life race on by. Don't allow opportunities and blessings placed in front of you to go unnoticed. You don't want to reach a place at the end of your life where you have regrets wishing you would've gone after something or taken a risk on what you desire. One of my exes initially went after me due to the fear of not ever seeing me again. This was on our last day of school where everyone was leaving, so it was now or never seeing me again. That fear was strong enough that propelled enough confidence and drive for my ex to come after me. Granted, they're my ex now for other reasons, but there are no regrets. We still speak highly of one another today.

I've always been a fan of the fearless and the courageous, even if they know they'll fall flat on their face. I love seeing anyone walk through fire no matter what because nothing holds them back. They stand in their soul's power. If they fall, they pay no mind and get back up and keep going as if it's no big deal. They're fearless and continue to stand strong in the face of any setbacks or calamity.

Mastering fearless confidence on Earth can be challenging with the endless toxic negative energy being darted at you from all angles. Sometimes you create that negativity with the power of your own mind. Your worries and fears are unfounded since in the end all is always well. In Heaven, all souls are fearless and confident. There is no lower energy that permeates their aura like it does on Earth.

Archangel Michael –
The Extractor of Fear

The Archangel Michael is God's right hand security general that oversees all beings, including Warrior of Light's, all archangels, and angels. Many Warriors of Light souls have Archangel Michael around them since he is one of the strongest most fearless beings in the Heavens. He might assist with extracting fear from a soul while helping them to rise to confidence when their lower self gets in the way. He is also their protector to ensure they are not harmed by anyone. Warrior of Light's tend to invite in antagonism from the lower evolved that feel threatened by their natural ability to stand in fearless, assertive, confidence full time. For that matter, it is beneficial to have Archangel Michael in your house to extract the lower energies out of your vicinity. Anyone can call on him when experiencing fear or an attack from lower energies.

Archangel Michael is the loudest entity I've ever come across throughout my life. He is the only entity louder than God, while stretching to appear as tall as 30 to 40 feet and sometimes taller to make his presence known. He is often depicted in artwork as standing on or holding down a hideous monstrous devil like creature without effort. This can be the Devil itself or the darkness of ego in individual souls.

Someone that might come off assertively overconfident and bold rubs the lower energies the wrong way. Archangel Michael is with me every day of my life and ironically this is his principal energy. Only the dark ego would be ruffled over another who exudes superhuman confidence. This is because one of the goals of the Darkness is to take down confidence or anyone that achieves.

Archangel Michael struts around almost like a boastful rooster alpha male. Calling him overconfident is too little of a word to describe his self-assurance. When he's not extracting lower energies and people away with his light sword, he's showing off like a male peacock. Sometimes the light around him bursts into a brightly colored light show for no reason at all except to show off the way a male peacock does. This is similar to Archangel Michael's basic nature when he's not diving into battle fearlessly for God.

Call upon Archangel Michael for intervention when you are drowning in fear, anxiety, self-doubt, or lacking in confidence.

People believe what they want to believe and there is nothing you can do about it. Thinking in a limited way is the kiss of death. Communicating with any angel or archangel is communicating with God. They are His arms and hands, so even if you don't feel you are communicating to God, you are. The best parts of the human soul are of God. The darkness of ego is not. You can't run away from God. Michael isn't more superior than God since he is of God. Michael is so powerful and loud that he comes off more superior than God, even though they are one in the same. This soldier angel is present in all of the Heavens in a big way!

Archangel Michael has been around popping up

over the centuries, but is now more present more than ever. The various reasons are that the Darkness is particularly heightened due to how rapidly it spreads through technology, which is why Michael has called on souls to come into this lifetime to fight the darkness of ego that exists in others. There are also more people on the planet, which equates to more minions for the Darkness to govern. And there are more people today that have become hip to spiritual pursuits and are need of Archangel Michael.

If you're experiencing a negative entity hanging around you, call on Archangel Michael and request that he bring the entity into the light. If you're feeling enormous fear, then bring in Archangel Michael to help lift you into bold confidence. Know that you are more powerful than you might give yourself credit for. Rise to the task of becoming the natural born fearless warrior soul you were made to be.

CHAPTER TWO

*Stand In Your
Divine Soul Power*

Finding that space of fearless confidence can be generated within the pilot light part of your soul that is ignited when you partner up with the Divine. You may call this the Divine, God, the Universe, Spirit, Energy, the Light. It's all the same thing regardless of the label used. This partnership enables you to efficiently stay on your higher self's soul path knowing when to make a move or to take a step back and have patience.

You are just as deserving of blessings, abundance, and success as any other soul being is. There is enough room on the planet for every single soul to experience success. There is always enough to go around. Everyone does and says things in their own way. They all have the ability to showcase their unique talents with their distinctive styles. It's interesting that the human ego prefers that everyone be a clone of them from having the same viewpoints, interests, and values across the board. It is the individual differences between each soul that is their winning card. Avoid listening to anyone that attempts to stop you from going after your life purpose or goals. They might tell you that you're not qualified or that you're not as gifted as someone else. When someone tells you that you're not qualified, they subconsciously mean that it is they who are not qualified. If I listened to all of those negative criticisms, then I never would've accomplished the things I did throughout my life. In the eyes of God, you are just as qualified as anyone else. When you accomplish what you set out to do, then you move into the space of being fueled by the Divine.

When you listen to the voices of your ego, the Darkness in your mind or in other people, then you will ensure you remain stuck. The goal of the Darkness is to attempt to stop you from accelerating and achieving success. You want to stomp the Hell out of that Darkness when it attempts to get in your way. When your feet hit the floor each morning the Darkness of Hell should shake. Your soul's success is not dependent on other people's opinions of you. When you partner with God, there is no telling what you can accomplish. You soar upwards into that space of fearless confidence that can only be generated through your connection with Him.

You go to a spiritual empowerment event to listen to five different guest speakers on motivation. They all enjoy talking about the same goal and content, but they're each discussing it in their own way. This indicates how everyone has something to offer surrounding the same topic, because not everyone says or does things in the same way. One speaker might not interest you, but they will interest someone else. The same goes for anyone in any field. One rock singer is different from another and appeals to the same or a different audience. There is enough room for everyone to contribute their talents in their authentic and original way.

In today's world post technology, one of the positives of having access to the Internet is that it has given many talented people various opportunities to showcase their talents had they had not access to get online. Many businesses have closed up physical stores, but kept their business thriving through online sales. Many have been moving into starting up their own successful self-employment business, while others have been transitioning into working from home either part or full time. This has resulted in more productivity, a calmer lifestyle, less stress, better health, and more energy.

There was this motivational YouTube video of this 18-year-old guy who was selling enough product online that he could do that full time. He explained that he doesn't have to take a full time nine to six corporate office day job that he'll end up despising because he does so well with this Internet business. Sometimes he walks along the beach on a Tuesday afternoon when no one is there because they're all at their soul crushing corporate day jobs. He loves that freedom of space to clear his mind without the crowds. He's able to do that because he sets his own hours and makes enough where he can afford to do that. He's not a millionaire or rich by any means, but he makes enough consistently and regularly to pay his rent and bills without worry. It gives him the luxury of working when he wants to rather than the rigid inflexible 9a-6p schedule that is the current norm. He gets more done in little time than it takes someone else in a corporate job. He also controls when he chooses to work.

There are more people than ever before that are moving into successful self-employment businesses. They started out by supplementing their income by taking a side day job while building their business on their downtime. You just want to do your best to look for a day job that makes you smile enough to not feel stressed and worried, otherwise that energy will carry over to the side hobby you've been working at building. It's still understood that sometimes you have to suck it up and take any day job. This is a physical life that requires money for physical survival necessities. When you are doing that you are ensuring that you and your family are taken care of. This is getting you in the habit of taking responsibility and being disciplined, which are winning traits that will be applied and carried over to all aspects of your life from personal to a professional self-employed business.

The sole cause of abundance blockage is fear. This fear can prevent someone from building a career out of their hobby. There are endless stories of someone finding their purpose, passion and hobby that wound by turning that into full time work where they can make survivable income off of. Some people will stay in what they perceive to be a dead end job for fear of biting the bullet and taking a risk to walk away and go after their life purpose work. You should never walk away from a job unless you know it's practically safe to do so. This means you are prepared for the worst-case scenario that could entail you not finding another job.

The best way to move your passion into a financially independent career is to work on it on the side while you have the security of your current job. Devote at least a small amount of work each day towards your side passion career, so that you don't feel as if you're wasting your life at a job you despise. The benefits to doing that are if it's your passion, then it doesn't feel like work. It also gives you something positive to look forward to each day knowing you have this back up plan you're working on. If one day you suddenly lose your job due to being laid off or fired, then at least you have this passion career on the side you had been working on. It just may give you the push to dive into it at full force once regular day job employment ceases to exist. It's never too late to think about and plan potential opportunities for your future today. You don't know where you'll be in ten or twenty years. The stable job with the security and the benefits can end with the snap of a finger. This has been happening a great deal more than it ever has.

Allow Your Confidence To Break Out

There are some that prefer you to be meek about your accomplishments. They see boasting about what you've done makes you come off as if you have a big ego or that you're a narcissist. The "narcissist" word grew to be an overused trendy social media term that has been tossed around with reckless abandon without truly understanding the psychological definition. Typically, those that complain or attack others that are higher achievers haven't accomplished much, so it feels like those that have attained many things are rubbing it in. Those who go out there and achieve what they set out to do are so busy in that energy of achieving that to stoop lower to complain, criticize or attack becomes beneath them. Talking about what you've accomplished and the hard work you've put in to making something happen is not arrogant. It's stepping into your confidence over your Divine given gifts, abilities and talents. Being a people pleaser doesn't work. Focus on the guidance you receive from above and you'll never be led astray.

Confidence is not a dirty word or trait to have. People fall in love with those that are confident over those that are weak. When a man or woman strides through a room head held high with a smile, then that is what attracts in others that glance over with a smile intoxicated by that confidence. They want to engage with that energy rather than a negative pessimist with low self-esteem that negatively critiques everything you say or do. To a higher vibrational soul the confident person is admirable as it shows you have goals, passion, and drive. It indicates that you're a hard worker, strong, and you get things done.

Warrior-like go-getters are attracted to other go-getters. Those looking to be inspired are attracted to those go-getters as it inspires them. When you persevere and accomplish your dreams and you succeed, then this is marvelous in the eyes of those that enjoy feeling inspired and motivated. It gives others hope that they can do it too. They know if they set their mind to it and work hard, then they will reach their destination.

When talking about your accomplishments with anyone whether it's in a job interview or with a friend, don't worry about coming off too assertive. Shout what you've accomplished from the rooftops and don't be fearful about it. Own what you created and fought to make happen. I received all of the previous jobs I did throughout the film business with the heavy talent in that industry due to this assertiveness that dominated the interview meeting. Each person that hired me had felt that this is someone that gets stuff done and we need something like that here.

When someone shouts their accomplishments from the highest mountain, then it isn't long before a negative beaten person will feel low, envy, or disdain about that. This pushes them to complain that the other person is not qualified, conceited, arrogant, or a narcissus, instead of admiring that confident quality in that person to go against the grain and tackle their passions. Use others accomplishments to motivate you to rise into who your soul is and shout that from the rooftops, rather than trying to spin it into something negative. Negative reactions typically come from jealousy and envy buried deep in the subconscious of the human ego.

Envy is a deadly emotional toxin because it pulls you under causing the Darkness to take over, envelope, drown, and suffocate you in that envy. Sometimes the envy might be due to jealousy, other times someone isn't jealous, but just a miserable person in general. They may have lived a life where others ignored them, so they will find fault with everyone and everything that is going after their dreams. No matter the context and whether it is jealousy or envy, all of those negative emotions are abundance blocks, since any form of negative emotion, feeling, or thought creates a block to blessings.

There is also the other kind of envy you may know about, which is generated in your heart. This is where you're not a bad person, but you have been working hard in life, and you're not seeing any positive results, traction, or movement, then you see someone else do what you had been doing for years and they shoot upwards across the map. You notice something like that happen and it ends up creating envy in you. You feel beaten down by it because your work is exceptional, you're gifted, accomplished at what you do, and you work so hard. You see someone with little experience or whom you might feel is not qualified necessarily, but they put something out and it attracts in the massive abundance. This will kick anyone on the sidelines wondering when your turn will come.

In those moments there isn't anything you did to attract that. Everyone has a different timeline as to when things pan out the way they're supposed to. It's important to do your best to stand strong in faith knowing that everyone's timing for things is different.

Affirm, "I am just as qualified as that person is. I'm glad that they are being blessed and by the way I'm in that line too!"

Research other success stories in the field of your interest in tips and inspiration.

A friend of mine went to a wedding with someone he was dating. He and his date found they were comparing themselves to the guests. The guests appeared to be advanced by the life status they achieved in both of their eyes. This friend explained that everyone at the wedding was accomplished and successful. They were also around the same age as he and his date. After the wedding, he and his date talked about it and felt like they were so far behind compared to the successful wedding patrons.

Comparing yourself to others can bring your vibrational energy down. Whether it's I'm better than you or you're better than me. Feeling like someone is better than you pulls you down harder because of the despair, disappointment, and frustration energy associated with it. You are not above or below me, because we are the same. Everyone has their own gifts and talents to offer to humanity for the greater good. Even if it's in the same genre you're interested in. Every single person has a distinctively unique way of offering those gifts and talents that will appeal to someone out there.

Working so hard and feeling as if you're getting nowhere fast can take its toll on you. You continue to struggle while others around you will try something and hit instant success. You might find yourself getting critical not understanding why. You might think lower energy words like, "They're younger than I, have almost little to no work experience, and they're better looking than I am...."

This can easily cause a combination of depression and envy. There is no set time frame for achieving success. Everyone has their own timeline of when things will come about. For some it may seem instant, while another will struggle for much longer. It doesn't mean you're less than or not talented enough. Sometimes it's the more talented and gifted that take the longer way around to see the abundance flowing into their life effortlessly. They're gaining more knowledge and experience that others don't have through that longer process. It's like the Tortoise and the Hare story. The Tortoise moved slower, but ended up surpassing the Hare in the end in that fairy tale.

It's been known at this point that I started my

work life in the film business when I was twenty-three years old working for a movie star actress at her company. All good blessings came down from that point where it opened more doors and job offers. I still receive notes from upcoming generations in their teens and young adulthood reaching out to me to ask how I got into the film business. Because the role I was brought in to do was difficult and considered rare for the age I was at during the time. They're trying to get in as well too. It was also during a time when Movie Stars existed and the public didn't have a connection with the remaining ones like they may have now due to the Internet, Instagram, and social media.

It took me seven years to get into the film business. I knew I would get in when I was sixteen, but it wasn't until I turned twenty-three when I finally got that lucky phone call out of the blue that changed my life. That was one of many major turning points and crossroads in my life. Getting in was persistence, passion, and dedication, but it was also a stroke of Divine luck and constant prayer. It was one call amidst it all that changed my life and cracked open the abundant door. I always say getting in was luck, but staying in was talent. That goes for anything anyone does. I came from a poor background and no access to resources, but I did have fearless assertive confidence when it came to getting that important job.

Stay strong; remain faithful, and full of hope, as you forge ahead undeterred by anything the darkness throws at you. Everyone is moving at their own pace. Feeling frustration over the lack of results can make you want to give up and throw in the towel, but keep going and stay focused on your purpose and mission. Avoid comparing your trajectory to someone else's because your talents are needed. You'll get there if it kills you. Your drive is your winning card, so don't allow someone else's success to squash what you are working on. Instead allow that to help you feel inspired and motivated to work even harder.

A healthy ego shines through when you are confident in your gifts, talents, and abilities while not shying away from announcing it to the Universe. The meek don't get far in this cutthroat world it's been learned, so allow the confident part of your soul to come out of that submissive side and allow it to shine its vibrant light into the ethers. Visualize that light expanding and growing more blinding than you can imagine that it blasts everything away in its wake. This is how powerful your soul light is back home in Heaven. While it may be ferociously beautifully strong on the Other Side, that light is still within your soul. It is simply contained inside the temporary physical body you've inhabited this lifetime. This light can still fluctuate and expand and contract as it does back home while within your body. It can get crushed under the weight of the Earth's energy density and the darkness of ego, but you have enough power to let the light out in an explosion that it breaks apart this darkness at your own will.

Self-Esteem and Self-Love

One of the other traits so many battle with today is low self-esteem. This wasn't always the case, but since the rise of social media giving everyone a voice it also amplified that low self-esteem in destructive ways. People growing up today are finding they keep comparing themselves to others on social media. He's beautiful with ripped abs and she's got a killer stunning body. Is this what we've allowed human life to become? A competition over who is better than someone else? Qualities that become non-existent the second you die. That sounds like an awfully long waste of time to be preoccupied with. Regardless, it seems to be inescapable because it is in your face every time you go online. You can't help it, you see it and you are brought down. This was going on before the Internet where magazines were airbrushing people to the point they were too perfect. Society was comparing themselves to the models on those covers not realizing that it's all lighting, make up, and hair people that make it all look good. It's also why actors have admitted it's difficult for them to watch themselves on screen. They'll nitpick and critique how they looked as well as their performance.

Talking with this body builder at the gym one day, the conversation moved into vanity. He commented that I seemed exceptionally fit, although I disagreed explaining that I like taking care of myself, but I don't personally see it. I then added that he was. He said, "Oh no, I don't see it in myself either. I think I have that body dysmorphia something or rather."

That kicked off a discussion into how people view themselves differently than the way others do. I was surprised to find that even though to others he appeared built, muscular, and physically fit, that he didn't see that at all. His personal view of himself is skewed to an unrealistic level. This was one person out of numerous people that I've conversed with over what they perceive to be flaws in themselves. I've also discovered that those who might be considered off the charts good looking battle with it more than others. This was a surprising revelation to learn.

In the past, I've discussed the process of external upkeep. Some body builders are extremely muscular to the point that others have explained it can be too much. They don't see themselves that way, so they continue pumping more iron than necessary that it becomes an unhealthy obsession. This has also been seen with some that partake in plastic surgery. Constantly having plastic surgery to the degree they become unrecognizable. They go beyond more than what was originally needed.

How about those that have spent enormous amounts of money to look like a celebrity. They've paid anywhere from $20,000 to a $100,000 to change their appearance to match a famous person. You have to wonder where someone's mind is at on the self-esteem scale when you drop that kind of money for something that superficial. It falls in line with other toxic addictions. There is a lack of self-love for who you are. This is different than the basic aesthetic grooming beauty upkeep one enjoys like facials, skin-care, hair-care, physical workout training, etc. Meanwhile, there are children that live in some kind of abusive impoverished situation with no funds to help them.

There is what could be considered genuine flaws to work on, such as if you're someone that has rage anger issues. Calling it a flaw may be the wrong word to describe it, and using the word challenge could be more appropriate. This particular kind of flaw or challenge is one you could admit, "I have anger issues. I'm aware of it and I have been working on trying to control it more."

That's a different kind of challenge that can be worked on to improve yourself. What you might perceive to be a flaw in your appearance and looks is subjective. Learn to love everything about you. You change the things you're able to change, and you love and accept the areas that absolutely can never be improved. Steer away from comparing yourself to others. In God's eyes you are a radiant beautiful being that He is already impressed with.

Humanity is gravely obsessive over their physical appearance because the ego in humankind harshly judges one another by what they look like. The perception of who is considered beautiful or good looking would be vastly different if people saw one another's soul instead of the physical vessel they temporarily inhabit. Relationships would last longer because people would be merging together based on soul attraction rather than physical attraction, even though I understand that physical attraction helps at first, but that's only the start of coming together. Physical attraction fades no matter how good looking someone is. When you're younger you base the quality of a potential love partner solely on their physical attractiveness to you. As you grow older and more mature, the quality of a potential love partner is based on personality chemistry and the companionship factor.

There would be less of an obsession to try and garner false attention through perfecting your exterior and more work done on your interior. Raising your consciousness and awareness level can help in rising above the superficial and diving beneath the surface to get to the root of who someone truly is. It can help you dive into getting to know who you are too. Those hyper obsessed with their bodies, selfies, attention, and constant physical exterior adoration aren't fans of that kind of talk. They take it as an attack, even though the message is a generality to smarten up and dive beneath the superficiality. One needs a healthy dose of spiritual saving if they're more consumed with vanity than penetrating the depths of all things beyond.

This isn't saying not to do your best to take care of yourself and look good in the areas you are able to, nor is it saying that there is anything wrong with finding yourself or someone physically attractive. It's about the borderline obsessiveness of being consumed wholly by your looks and basing your existence on whether or not your body is worshipped by others. External validation is a shallow goal. Fixing yourself up in the areas you are able to has been shown to help build up confidence, but you don't want to fall too deep into basing your confidence on how you look and what you have, since the confidence is within you regardless of how you look.

I've been just as guilty of the selfie craze having done the muscle flexing selfies, although I was never doing it as much as others and it's rare when I do that anyway. I've had people ask me to check out their Instagram page. I head over there and notice their entire Instagram is nothing but hundreds of every selfie of them that you can imagine scrolling all the way down. It's concerning to see how deep they've fallen into the obsession of superficiality, attention, and adoration. They use their body and looks to gain false attention. They're not promoting a product associated with their body such as fashion or fitness, but are just seeking love from others. What might be even more disconcerting is they get that attention, which is likely why they continue doing it. Thousands of people are liking and splattering each photo with attention, but it's shallow attention.

I've also run those social experiments where I've purposely put up a photo of me fully clothed, which garners little attention. One week later I then put up the opposing shot, which is me shirtless and suddenly the image skyrockets to the top of the trending mark. The approving comments, likes, and messages in my in-box flood. Meanwhile, I'm disappointed to see the experiment worked. I'm aware how shallow humanity is by their opposing reactions to each shot. I've been out there and tested everything discussed. When you have self-love for yourself, then the desire for constant external adoration isn't looked-for.

Self-love and gratitude are magical elements to incorporate into your life that help in pushing the abundance door wide open. This positive thinking isn't news when it comes to attracting in abundance. This is to hammer home the feel good feelings to reach into ones psyche where you can feel more inspired. This is to experience contentment and optimism about where you are currently at and what's to come. It is to praise how far you've come and how hard you've worked. Give yourself the credit for what you've accomplished to date.

Rapper Snoop Dogg received his star on the Hollywood Walk of Fame in 2018. I fell in love with his speech because he praises himself and gives himself the credit:

"Last but not least, I want to thank me for believing in me. I want to thank me for doing all this hard work. I want to thank me for having no days off. I want to thank me for never quitting. I want to thank me for always being a giver and trying to give more than I receive. I want to thank me for trying to do more right than wrong. I want to thank me for just being me at all times."

I chuckled because I thought it was amazing and brilliant. Some immediately get turned off or offended when anyone believes in themselves or props themselves up. They'll naively throw the ego or narcissistic word around with abandon. There is nothing wrong with applauding and giving yourself credit for the hard work you put in. You're the one doing the work, give yourself a round of applause! You can't rely on others to prop you up. Prop yourself up!

On one occasion, I was hanging with my former actress boss about three years into my employment with her. We were kicking back chatting about things. At one point I said, "I really have to thank you, because I could not have done all of these things I've done to date without your help and you opening that door."

She just point blank said with a lighthearted smile, "Oh stop, you did it yourself."

That forever stuck because I thought, "Actually you are right. I shouldn't be bowing down to others for the work I fought to do on my own."

External human validation isn't something I require, because I know my worth through source. I know who I am, what I can do, and what I've done. Believe in yourself and give yourself credit when you do good things. Praising yourself is considered self-love that lifts your vibration up into the vortex of attracting in more good stuff.

CHAPTER THREE

*Stomp Out the Darkness
of Fear, Gossip, and Anger*

There's nothing more paralyzing and detrimental to human beings than fear. Fear has plagued humankind since they first started inhabiting Earth. Fear blocks you from moving forward and prevents the positive flow of abundance. Fear can come in the disguise of worry, stress, depression, and anger. It will expand negative emotions and create madness depending on the case. Fear isn't just about fearing making a positive move in life. Fear resides in those that truly dislike groups of people. For instance, hate crimes against someone who is different than the antagonist generally begins to breed in the womb of fear. The antagonist might respond by saying, "I'm not afraid of them. I just don't like them."

Basically, they don't like anyone that falls into a particular demographic. This comes from a subconscious fear of coming across someone who isn't exactly like you. God throws everyone together on the same rock to learn tolerance, acceptance, and forgiveness. Those are some of the most difficult traits that people have trouble with conveying. This is clear due to how people stick with their own groups the same way they did on the elementary school playground. This is the innate primal human instinct, but it is not the soul part of you. The soul is inclusive, but the human ego is exclusive.

There were more people than not who were once prejudiced against race, then it became prejudice over anyone that had a same sex relationship. Once they realized that every other person they loved around them fit the description of people gay, then they gradually changed their tune realizing they made a mistake about their hatred and just didn't know any better. Now it's becoming increasingly common and accepted, but there are still those living in the stone ages with a limited view that have yet to gain love for those not like them.

Using Biblical text that was added in at a later date by superstitious fearful men isn't a good excuse, since God created all breathing life this way for a reason. God doesn't have hang ups about two souls in love with each other regardless of their gender. Love is what He desires to see, so in that instant when two souls are in love, He is pleased. God has disdain for those that express hatred over two souls in a committed love relationship, let alone disdain for those that display hatred on any level. If you have hatred in your heart, then there is no Divine energy existing in there. Jesus Christ was the same way. His complaint was over adultery and not about committed love between two souls.

Dive down deep as to why you don't like someone. Hating an entire group isn't valid because there are good and bad people in all groups. When you pull one person out of that group you despise and you're locked in a room with them to have a conversation, there is a greater chance that when you both leave that room you'll like them. If anything, you will both at least have a bit more compassion, respect, and understanding of them. The only way that will never work is if someone's consciousness is not raised. A limited consciousness permanently resides in darkness unable to break free. The darkness is where fear lives. In order to get over a prejudice you have about a certain class of people is to spend one on one time with them in a casual friendly setting.

I've conducted social experiments like this. This is where I've placed two people in a room together who are in opposition on the political spectrum. The intention of putting them in the room together was to get them to have friendly conversation outside of their personal political choices. Nine times out of ten they generally ended up liking each other, or at least respecting each other despite their personal political values. The exceptions are those that are entirely extreme and rigid that no light or tolerance has room to enter the picture. This is the current state of the universe today. There is zero Divine clarity and psychic foresight within hatred or negativity of any kind. When you take the time to get to know someone different from you, then eventually you come to a greater more compassionate understanding of that person.

You've likely witnessed people attacking another person over their personal views. This does nothing to change that person. Seeking to understand them and have a cordial sit down conversation with them is more likely to gain some measure of respect. This is not always the case amongst those rare exceptions, but in many paradigms it is. If you already know they can't be reasoned with, then wish them well, bless them on their path to enlightenment, let it go and walk away.

Fear energy is also one of the major culprits to blocking the flow of positive abundance and blessings in one's life. It doesn't matter if the fear is over achieving your goals or fear that causes you to despise an entire group of people. It is still fear energy in the eyes of the Universe. Fear lives within the darkness of a soul's ego. Fear is responsible for the chaos energy that forever surrounds the planet when humankind is operating from a low vibration. Fear will make you doubt yourself and bring on baseless worry energy.

Doubts and worry that you will not achieve or succeed what you desire stems from fear. When that happens, then you need a healthy dose of inspiration that can be found in empowering music, books, or films. This is one of the positives of entertainment, which was created to help people forget about their troubles, help them to lighten up, or give them a dose of inspiration. Balanced entertainers that remain neutral on their personal values while in the public eye don't always get enough credit for this goal at times.

The alternative rock song *High Hopes* by *Panic at the Disco* sings, "I had to have high hopes for a living. Shooting for the stars when I couldn't make a killing. Didn't have a dime, but I always had a vision. Didn't know how, but I always had a feeling I was going to be that one in a million."

Listen to empowering music with positive lyrics that help motivate you. Watch movies about those that came from nothing and made something with their life. Rags to riches stories can be incredibly inspiring. People that had nothing and struggled with little to no money, but soon overcame that and made something with their life. They might be films like *Erin Brockovich, People Vs. Larry Flynt,* or *Joy.*

Erin Brockovich was a regular person trying to make ends meet. She found a cause that moved her and was mainly interested in uncovering it. The financial abundance ended up coming in, even though that was not her concern when fighting for the underdog.

The Founder, another rags to riches film that stars Michael Keaton, was based on the true story of Ray Kroc, the guy that created the McDonald's fast food chain. Opinions on him are across the board from people that loved him and those that loathed him. The point of this was that he was an unsuccessful salesperson, but somehow struck gold when he found something great in the McDonald's formula for fast food. He ended up rising up the ranks to major never-ending financial success.

Watching those rags to riches type films can leave you feeling as if you were injected with newfound inspiration and optimism. Joyful experiences can help you get into a positive state, but so does aligning with God and Spirit. Putting your trust and faith into the universal heavenly forces above is better than any material abundance that can be offered.

Many successful known entertainers admit to having self-doubts or fear, which humanizes and helps them to be relatable to their audience. They fear they're not that good or that they'll be found out that they're no good. They are good at what they do, they are popular, and at the top of their game, but they're also human and have human emotions that their success is a fluke.

It helps to have some perspective that everyone experiences doubts or worries, but don't let that cripple you to the point of non-movement. You rise above it and keep forging forward making the most of what you can do while you are here. You may as well try, because what else do you have to lose?

Turn Anger Into Positive Action

Manifesting fearless assertive confidence can hit a threshold where your higher self has lost control of the reigns allowing space for your ego to grab the steering wheel taking you on Mr. Toad's Wild Ride. This confidence begins to expand and burn rapidly out of control driving your ego into fury and anger. The ego is unstable always residing in some constant state of fear, which can manifest into anger. Fear is not always apparent to what it actually is. The fear can be fearful of being trampled on, pulled down, not reaching success. You do whatever you can to ensure success that you begin to act out erratically due to this fear. Every person on the planet has the fear and anger within them that comes out in various ways. Depending on your overall character and nature, your anger temperament will be different than another person's. The way you react in anger will vary compared to someone else. Is the Dalai Lama or the Pope running around bullying people on the sidewalk, verbally attacking people on social media, or starting fist fights for no reason? They have a different centered assertive way of channeling that anger positively.

All forms of anger are toxic putting stress on your health and body, but that doesn't mean you're supposed to pretend to be happy when you're faced with challenging circumstances that break your equilibrium or drive you to fury, such as when someone betrays your love and trust. Even if you pretend that you're fine and put on the false face, within the embers of your soul is revealed to be your true face, the mirror held up to the Heavens. It is your body, your Spirit team, and God that know how your consciousness truly feels. It's your senses they read and instantly pick up on that have far greater energy than the pretend face you're putting on for others. It's what is in your heart that is read and not how much money you have in the bank, what kind of car you drive, or the awards you have under your name. It is your character and heart the angels see and know to be true over any pretense shown. It is how you choose to act before you achieve your desires.

This is also why you cannot get away with a lie with any spirit being the way you can with another person, unless of course one has a high degree of Claircognizance (clear knowing). Claircognizant beings tend to psychically know when someone is lying, even if they don't call them out on it. Most of the time depending on how severe or harmless the lie is they just keep it to themselves. If everyone increased their psychic abilities innate within them since their soul's conception, then they would be able to detect things like when a media story is exaggerated or produced with the indirect intention of riling your ego up. A raised consciousness also helps in peering beneath the surface and being proactive rather than reactive.

Look at what it is that you continuously jump to anger about. This is one of the many clues as to what your many life purposes are. The next step is to channel that anger positively for the greater good. For example, if you always get angry over those who toss trash everywhere but in a trashcan, then use the anger constructively by seeking out ways to prevent that from happening. Those that get upset over anyone dumping trash in the ocean might be someone who chooses to join an organization like Greenpeace to fight to keep Earth clean. They are turning their anger into positive action.

Someone cut you off in traffic and you immediately understandably rise to anger, but then depending on who you are, you hopefully get over it within a minute and move on. I was biking down a hill once and into a bike line that crosses over a lane for cars that turns right. It's not a busy street, but one car whipped around in front of me out of nowhere to cross over to turn right. They were driving recklessly. If they had accidentally braked I would've flown into their car. That would drive anyone to anger because it was obvious in that scenario that the driver is an example of an aggressive erratic impatient driver that will eventually cause a major accident due to this angry driving. Sadly as many have informed me and I've witnessed this is not uncommon. This is what happens when you give an ego a machine to control and drive around. It then becomes a weapon that the ego feels temporarily invincibly safe within the same way a negative toxic commenter feels safe hiding behind an alias online to type out obscenities and attacks at people all day long. These are false ways that confidence is felt since these technological methods give the illusion of making you feel confident temporarily.

It's the same as mobs that mobilize to protest and enact violence on others they disagree with rather than coming together to fight poverty or child abuse. In those moments they are temporarily confidently empowered behind the safety of a group, which isn't authentic confidence. True healthy confidence is generated within by having a strong faith-based connection with the Divine. It operates in a composed, compassionate, and assertive manner rather than a bulldozing violent one.

How about if you discover the person you devoted yourself to in a committed relationship or marriage had been unfaithful to you, or pulled the rug out from underneath you by leaving the connection. The anger felt with that will be greater than the anger over someone cutting you off in traffic. Except in this case the anger turns to sadness and grief, but as hard as it would be to accept it is the ego that is bruised. It can be challenging to get to a place where one comes to the realization that the unfaithful wasn't deliberately trying to hurt you. This doesn't mean you have to be best pals, but part of spiritual growth is getting to that place where you can accept that this is that person's journey and it has nothing to do with you. You are in a different place in life that is more aligned with someone on that same frequency.

For others they'll remain in the epicenter of anger becoming hardened and indefinitely bitter. You'll develop fear that every potential future relationship will result in that person doing the same thing. In that sense, you continuously create the reality that this is what is to be. It plays out in the exact same way over and over again with future mates. That is until you choose to break the pattern and make character adjustments to prevent the same lessons from being repeated indefinitely.

Fear is one of the biggest abundance blocks that continues to destroy humanity on so many levels. When you have fear of anything in life, then that fear creates a blessing block. This can be fear of the end of the world being near or fear over anything associated with the media or politics. Anything connected to the word fear affects your consciousness, which then affects the flow of positive abundance.

Most of the things you fear and want to run from are the tools you're intended to use to help improve and transform your soul. There is a reason you endure difficult circumstances, whether it's a job you currently don't care for or a relationship connection that didn't end well. You were gaining wisdom, knowledge, and skills while in those circumstances to take with you to the next venture. Every experience I had gave me additional tools and traits that would be needed for my next mission and so on. All experiences you have are not just life changing growth qualities gained, but they happen so that you can apply it to future endeavors.

Take any anger and channel it positively through action. This action should be intended to fix whatever it is you're angry about, otherwise let it go. Being angry at a circumstance that took place or at someone else isn't going to make them change. They're off busy happily doing their thing while you're at home bitter and irritated marinating in that toxic cesspool energy that only attacks your state of well-being.

If you're angry about a particular issue, then stand up and speak out in ways that can benefit others positively. This isn't to be confused with vocally complaining or gossiping about something, or ranting and raving on social media, all of which is lower vibrational negative energy that does nothing to benefit anyone at all ever. If something is bothersome and you feel the need to vent or complain, then turn the words into action statements that can progress matters. If you're upset about a political policy, then tell Congress as many of my friends have done. Rather than posting daily toxic complaints, they're getting dressed up in their Sunday best and standing before Congress to present their case to stay focused and push a particular bill through for approval. If one is legitimately passionate about a particular issue, then they will find ways to change things by going through the right channels where it will make more of a difference than a little social media rant.

If you're truly interested in rising above an issue, then you will communicate in ways that will resolve it so that you can continue moving forward fearlessly instead of remaining stuck in the quick sand of toxicity. Honor your higher self's truth and wishes, which includes speaking your truth with assertiveness and compassion.

Be fearless and stand up for yourself and ask for what you want, whether it is from your Spirit team or those in life that can help you. This can be for something like getting another job to finding the right love partner.

Dissolve all of the layers of negativity you've accumulated so that you can bring that part of your life to closure. Start a bright new chapter each day with a clean slate vibrantly informed. Create more suitable solutions for yourself that will make you infinitely happier in the end. Never do or say anything just to make someone feel better if it makes you feel less than your stellar self by doing so. Channel anger positively to get your soul back into Divine alignment where you are in an assertive, centered focused space.

Dangers of Critical Gossip

Avoid gossiping and negatively talking about others and what you feel they did to you or how you feel about them. When you find you're doing that, wrap it up and shift the words to positive action oriented words and how you plan to bring things to a resolve. The same goes for those that criticize you. You will be criticized at some point in your life if you haven't already. This is whether you offer services to the public or someone you know harshly criticizes you in a way that is non-constructive with malice intentions. Many have offered different ways of handling that from examining what they're saying, to engaging with them calmly and positively, to sending them love and light. The best way to handle someone like that is to ignore them. You don't engage with someone ranting negatively at, about, or around you. This is the same way you avoid inviting any negative spirit into your aura. There is no positive benefit in engaging with dark energies.

The darkness of ego is the culprit behind negative moods and thoughts. When you allow the light to come cracking in, then that is a sign your higher self is taking back the control. The ego is a dreadful culprit in getting in the physical world's way of true happiness.

Refrain from using world events as a reason to fall into the lower energies of blame, gossiping, and politicizing. Human trauma of any kind can shake one's faith. Don't allow any human tragedy to consume you to the point of fear that you disconnect from the Divine. Free will choice and the darkness of ego have no connection with source.

There will be a natural cycle of uncomfortable emotions that you'll endure, play out, and move through until you've reached that space of having forgiveness for anyone that upset you. This is in order to graduate from that and move forward and onward in your life back into fearless assertive confidence.

Picking Your Battles

One of the other greater challenges many have is maintaining a sense of serenity and peace. This includes getting along with people that are different from you. You're presented with varying circumstances that can easily generate upset. When this happens, then be mindful that it's happening. Your soul was born peaceful and without judgment of those different from you. If someone is happy living their life and they're not hurting anyone, then it's no ego's place to interfere with that. This also doesn't mean you allow someone to bully or run you over. You have to be hyper-vigilant and aware as you navigate Earthly creation whenever other people are around. Many sleepwalk throughout their Earthly life. They move through the same daily routine activities they were trained to do by others early on. Some never work to improve, enhance, and awaken their true consciousness spirit, but merely go along with the popular fads and lingo of that time period they grew up in.

A lower state of being seems to be easier to attain than achieving a higher state of being. The irony is most people that are in a low vibrational state wish they had the latter. They find it challenging to reach a higher state of being. When you're angry about something, then the last thing on your ego's mind is not about re-centering as quickly as possible. It is about jumping into reaction instead of taking a step back to observe and evaluate what and why something is triggering you. Re-centering is the next step to take when you've fallen into a space of negativity or an angry reaction. This isn't asking you to deny your feelings of anger, since anger is one of the many emotions that exist in humankind, but it is an emotion that comes from the ego. You want to find the source of what is causing that anger, then look at the grander picture of what you're angry about to see if it's misplaced or not. Nine times out of ten it tends to be misplaced.

Every hour spent angry is a waste of time. Take that anger and channel it positively through action that can fix or correct whatever it is your angry about otherwise work on letting it go. Being angry with someone else isn't going to change or enlighten that person. They're off happily doing their thing while you're at home brooding over something they did, said, or anything about them. This can be someone you know personally, a public figure, or a stranger.

Some tend to get angrily riled up over something a public figure said or did in the media. This does nothing to change that person and it doesn't resolve anything. You don't know them and you're not in their house having a conversation with them. Instead your aura marinates in that toxic cesspool energy that doesn't hurt the target. It hurts you and your well-being, while simultaneously blocking heavenly spirit guidance from coming in.

Many fall into the allure of posting repetitive complaints on their social media accounts that ultimately wastes time and spreads the dark energies. The ego convinces you that you're being proactive, but darting negative complaints and words to someone isn't proactive but reactive. This dark energy flows into the cells of your body and gets lodged in there when improperly channeled. If someone was out of line with you, then take a moment to sit on that before responding if you have to respond. You'd be surprised how you can win over your opponent when you respond with assertive confidence rather than ruffled aggression.

If the anger is a daily pattern or left unchecked, then it can manifest into something more harmful, such as a breeding ground for future diseases and health issues. Due to the state of humanity today and its obsession with drama, this will cause an enormous amount of health issues, which will be seen in the later years. At press time the trend of posting negative rants on social media is really only about less than ten years old. It hasn't been going on long enough to notice the negative health repercussions, but these health issues are building within them now.

When you're in the epicenter of that developed hurricane of toxicity forming in and around you due to your own words, feelings, and thoughts, then it's difficult to be aware that you are. Dark energy blinds you to the truth for gain of witnessing your own downfall. When one falls into the deep seed of repetitive anger, then they are out of their minds and oblivious to how far down the rabbit hole they've fallen. If this is you, then you later realize that it's been one thing after another going wrong in your life while being unaware of how or why it grew at such an astronomical rate. The dangers can be seen in someone whose consciousness is on the cusp of expanding, otherwise the pattern will repeat indefinitely until death.

One way to counteract this dark energy is by

avoiding the gossip media. Stop seeking out salacious top trending headlines and social media posts designed to attract, entice, and lure you in. Avoid commenting and posting attacks wherever possible. The ego loves drama because it's designed to get you caught in its web preventing you from seeking out more positive activities to focus on that bring you into the epicenter of enlightenment. Use discernment and good judgment over what media is worth knowing and what is something that is out of your hands. I've found that most of it is unhelpful.

There are a number of people around me that don't get involved in gossip or media to the point that they really don't know what everyone is arguing about and they like it that way. Unless your job is a position that requires you to correct certain issues you're passionate about, then there is no benefit to joining in with the crowd to argue about the latest dramatic news story. The ones who don't agree with your values won't be positively influenced, so it's a time waster. Politicians do that to each other on Twitter behaving like Children, with other Children chiming in with their banter because they feel like they're being heard. All it creates is a bunch of time wasting non-productive noise where you're preaching to the choir or you're not. It's not changing anything of value. No one you're attempting to get on your side to agree with you are going to stop and say, "Oh you know what you're right. Thank you for attacking me in a tirade of curse words because I now see your point."

That's never happened in the history of negative

rants. Most of the time what people are arguing and gossiping about is forgotten within one to three days as another enticing headline flies to the top of the list to attract in their focus. It can take practice and enormous willpower to not be tempted to read certain types of content. That practice includes immediately knowing whether something is a gossip piece or an objective balanced news piece focused on straight neutral reporting. If every time you get riled up over media pieces put up by a particular news source, then it's time to step away from that source for awhile in order to get re-centered and re-directed on more important priorities that will ultimately bring you joy and peace.

The ego part of the soul gets riled up and angry in its own way. The trick is to catch it when it happens so that you resolve whatever it is that got a rise out of you. Learn to pick your battles and by quickly taking steps to bring that anger back down to the space of contentment again. This isn't about ignoring your anger and your feelings, but like everything connected to spiritual growth and evolvement you're growing more self-aware of the modifications you need to make. The more content you are, then the more confident you are.

Figuring Life Out As You Go

There is a difference between protesting against something that your values tell you to be wrong, as opposed to rebelling against someone else's sound judgment intended to prevent disaster or chaos from swallowing you up whole. All you can do is let that person figure it out the hard way. It can no doubt be frustrating because you care about that person and don't want to see them fall off that cliff, but in the end it's not up to you. This is their life and they need to stumble and fall on their own. If you spend all your days doing things for them, then they'll never learn anything. They might learn later in life or when it's too late long after you've gone. At that point, they have no other choice, but to find their own way solo.

If you're a parent or guardian of a child, then you have some measure of understanding of this. Especially when a child reaches a certain age where they gradually assert their independence and discover who they are as an individual. This means they will rebel even if what you're telling them is helpful. They may purposely defy you and head right for that cliff anyway just to spite you. It can be maddening to see someone you care about walking towards a cliff knowing there is nothing you can say that will stop them from that. The more you attempt to stop them, the more they carry on towards that cliff. The ego is a rebellious beast that will do what it wants when it wants.

A parent is guiding their child not necessarily to be strict, but because they know what will happen if the child makes an erratic decision. They know because they had gone through it themselves. There comes a point when you need to give someone else wiggle room to be free and discover the art of learning on their own.

A parent is essentially intended to be a guide the

way a spirit guide is for a soul. The guide isn't living the soul's life, but gently pointing them in the direction that will bring in the best results for their higher self. While doing this they and you ultimately leave the soul free reign to make the choice that sits most comfortably for them, even if it's a choice that will not be desirable in the end. God is much like a parent with all souls hoping to steer the soul away from danger and towards peace.

If a soul doesn't make mistakes, then how can it grow and evolve? Sometimes it can take someone months, years, or decades for the soul to realize that the way they've been doing things hasn't exactly been successful. That's the start of the change potentially happening within them and then the real work comes in. This change can come in as a call from God or the Divine. Receiving the awakened call is just the beginning, because then you have to put in the work.

The mind and heart are rarely in agreement with each other. Your heart longs for a particular person, job, or circumstance, but your mind talks you out of it. The rational mind loves to dance with the ego, otherwise known as the dance with the Devil. The ego resides in the mind intent on overriding and dominating the higher self. It will insist on doing what it wants to do regardless of what your heart is saying. The ego doesn't like back talk and will stomp its feet in a tantrum after you give it a challenging response that didn't back it up.

There is a reason circumstances take place beyond your control or current understanding. Life ebbs and flows, nothing stays the same, and not every soul sticks around with you throughout your entire Earthly life. Know yourself and learn to be independent of relying on anyone, except God and your angels for guidance.

None of the world drama that goes on matters in the end because every soul on the planet has a Divine plan attached to their consciousness. This is the case even if you cannot see that while in the moment. It is the responsibility and life quest of that soul to come to the conclusion of what their purpose and plan is on its own. No other being can inform them of what it is.

Some find they've given their power away to others, whether it's a friendship, relationship, or family member. There was a time in my late teens and early twenties when I was living hand to mouth with little to no money, but I pulled myself up and began working to take care of me. An example of giving your power away might be if ones partner takes care of things. This prevents you from being independent. Eventually a time comes where you feel suffocated and stuck wanting to move on, but you're unable to because your partner pays the bills and you haven't had a job in years. This makes you feel even more paralyzed and stuck.

You can get unstuck from giving your power away by taking steps to fix the circumstance. You rise up into that fearless assertive confidence within you and take back the controls. Once you find work and begin making your own money, then you are able to take steps to leaving the person you've given your power away to. This is no different than when you are a young person living under your parent's roof.   If you don't want to live in a situation forever, then you need to become an independent adult and do something about it by conjuring up Divine fearless confidence from within. Get a job, make money to survive, and find another place to move to.   You can't live life depending on someone else to save you. Take the bull by the horns and take control.

CHAPTER FOUR

Identify Blocks to Abundance and Blessings

It's beneficial to reach that place where you are grateful and thankful for what you have in the moment. It's a difficult task to accomplish when your soul knows what it desires next and sees no movement. I understand this frustration as I've been there too. What I have desired eventually has come to fruition, which is why I share those personal stories. It's to illustrate that I'm not spouting off random wisdom on a teabag, but have gone through the hard times myself on so many levels. I've gone through it and endured it, then found ways to conquer and overcome it. This includes from the incessant child abuse to the toxic addictions to cigarettes, alcohol, and drugs, to rising up the ranks behind the scenes in the entertainment business. The stories of what I've endured are numerous, but it's said to give someone else hope that is in those trenches right now. You can climb out of it with a strong confident will and determination. It will be a long running fight, but in the end, you'll reach that Promised Land.

One of the many teachings that Heaven has passed down to me is to feel grateful for what you have now. This state of being is what raises your vibration. The raised vibration is what brings in those desires you crave. The feeling grateful condition is of benefit to you because of the rewards that come with it. When you're feeling good, then more of that greatness comes into your life. When you feel lousy, pessimistic, and miserable, then it's as if it is one bad thing happening after another. What you put out is returned back to you and what you reap you sow. Plant the seeds of what you want now, and then on Divine timing watch it blossom into fruitful flowers and come to fruition. These are common metaphors because many have expressed to having tested out these theories with great success.

It is common sense that if you want a job, then you have to fill out job applications or send out your resume. No one is going to call you with a job offer if they don't know who you are or that you're looking for work. You want to win the lottery, then increase your chances by buying a ticket. These are basic examples of how the universe works. When you put a little action oriented effort, and you ask your Spirit team for assistance, then they meet you half way. It isn't enough to do all three, but you want to also feel optimistic, excitement, and gratefulness at the same time. Putting all of those traits together is a winning combination that will take you closer towards success instead of keeping you perpetually negative, pessimistic, and full of worry.

Whenever I would suggest anything to some people that could help positively change their life, they would respond with something negative. I would hear statements such as, "Oh they'll never hire me. They'll want someone thinner or younger. I'm not qualified."

I noticed the repetitive negative words being voiced. You have to want to fight for your life. Don't govern it based on what you think others want. You might be surprised to find that when you keep kicking a door that it will eventually be knocked down and you'll get that breakthrough at any age and no matter your qualifications, experience, or stats.

If there comes a point when you're helping someone else to make positive changes that you discover they're not interested in ever changing, then this is your cue to begin backing away. There is nothing more you can say that will break someone out of their monotony. It's been months and maybe even years of the same sad song being sung from that person. When in that negative state, the individual is not always putting in the work or asking for Divine intervention and help. How I obtained my past desires we're by stepping into confidence, asking for Divine help, and following the guidance they gave me by putting in the work through action. There were the naysayers and critics, but they will always be circling like gnats as you've likely come to experience yourself on occasion. You don't pay any attention to that and continue forging on with your purpose and goals living life for you.

Whenever there has been anything I wanted to accomplish, then I would have consistent excitement and optimism about it inside. There were the occasional doubts or worry that I would not obtain my goal, but those feelings were rare and miniscule. The feeling would only pop up once in a blue moon for a brief moment, then it would blow away just as fast. It was so infrequent that it did not dominate or rule me. I'd naturally and quickly move right back to optimism and in feeling grateful. I also had it in the back of my mind that I would keep trying to do what I wanted, because I wanted it bad enough. I frequently asked my Spirit team for assistance in prayer. I paid attention to what they were guiding me to do and then I took action and followed it. With hard work, passion, and persistence I eventually saw results begin to trickle in. There is no such thing as instant successes. It's a matter of little action steps each day that are bringing the success closer to you.

Sometimes the grateful state of mind is experienced by force such a less than stellar situation takes place in your life. You wish you weren't complaining so much because now things have grown worse. Those experiences are also designed to teach your soul gratitude and humility. It is by pushing you into a harder circumstance in order to see that during your previous repetitive complaining juncture that things were not as bad as they could be. Now they are worse in order to send your soul that wake up call to have more gratitude. You experience gratitude when you are aware that you may not be where you want to be yet, but you are grateful for the things that are working in your life. This is what opens up the doorway for blessings to enter the picture.

Constant complaining is a block preventing positive movement. Coming across someone who has it far worse than you do is something that can shake someone out of their negative rut. The guilt comes on for having complained repeatedly about how unhappy you are with where you're currently at. No one in Heaven wants to see you unhappy. They do want to help guide you out of it. You're not purposely being ignored since they're not cruel. There are steps that need to be taken to reach that space of happiness. There are also emotional traits such as gratitude and humility that need to be gained in the process. You are forced to be humble so that when the good stuff does come in you will be in a place to receive it in the right modest spirit.

Guilt is another trait that can block one from success. You feel a twinge of guilt that you are undeserving of good and this creates a block between yourself and your desires. I've had the slight guilt that would pinch me wondering if I was asking for too much. Luckily, those moments were rare since most of the time my basic nature is one of optimism.   Guilt also comes onto someone who feels they're being an imposition.   Someone sensitive with strong Clairsentient psychic channels might feel guilt when someone wants to help or do something nice for them.   It's merely a matter of catching yourself when you fall into a negative state, and then immediately work on shifting your mind's thoughts down a more positive and uplifting direction.

If the guilt were a reaction to how poorly you treated someone else, then you would work on shifting away from the guilt and make amends with the person you treated in a hurtful way.   This is by being aware of your surroundings and how you treat others.   You pay that karmic debt back by reaching out to that person to bury the hatchet from a place of compassion.   You consciously know that you want to make it right.   Once that's accomplished you move on to the next level.   It sounds contradictory to point out that you should not feel guilt, but you should also not feel nothing at all either, because then you're moving into sociopathic territory.   The trick is to find that middle ground where you're aware of how or what you've done to someone, but you're not drowning in the guilt.   Nor are you living in a state where you are unfazed by your behavior.

Some circumstances have barriers and blocks preventing you from experiencing the life you want. When you've admitted to the negative feelings you are allowing to plague you, then that is a great step towards reaching the breaking point where you're freed.   You become highly aware of what has caused these uncomfortable emotions. You've sacrificed your happiness to do what you feel is right. This is an amazing quality to have, but it's also time to begin the process of thinking of you first. There's nothing selfish about making sure that you're taken care of before anything or anyone else. If you're not taken care of, then it's difficult to take care of anyone else. Others may walk all over you and take advantage of your goodness when you display signs of being totally selfless with nothing in return. They don't all necessarily do that on purpose, which is where one must train them to treat you and others with respect. In general, they are typically not fully aware that this is how they're behaving.

As you remove the barriers that have been erected in front of you on your path, then your psychic Clair sense channels will begin to work at optimum levels. The negative feelings are creating these blocks. You're applauded when you make positive life changes, such as giving up or reducing certain addictions that cause these blocks. Sometimes that's not enough if the negative feelings are still there as that is also a block. This is partially why working on extricating negative thoughts and feelings is equally essential. You have a conscious and you're extremely aware of what's going on around you, so it's challenging to not be paying attention to it or noticing how you feel.

Unhealthy relationship connections are also a block. There can be some relationship healing that needs to take place. This includes forgiveness, letting go of blame, or any feelings of victimhood associated with a broken connection that continues to plague you.

Your mind and your body go through a work out with physical human life challenges. It can be super exhausting causing you to feel overwhelmed and stuck. All of these circumstances can create blocks in your way from obtaining good. Know that you do deserve good and are deserving of love.

These blocks can be removed by requesting heavenly assistance. Other ways are by taking frequent breaks throughout each day. This is taking at least fifteen minutes once a day where that time is solely for you. Find an area where it's not crowded with people and take regular walks. It can be to walk around the block, through a quiet nature setting, or strolling through a place where you know you won't feel assaulted by any harsh energy emitting off of others. This includes avoiding a busy street with cars racing by. You need quiet serenity in order to contemplate and commune with Spirit. Doing this will help you to clear your mind out, raise your vibrational state, and allow for great ideas on your next steps to flow in.

Allow your thoughts to wander while on these walks. Your thoughts may start off on the negative side over a circumstance that's been bothering you, or you'll be thinking about where you're at with your life. While being outside and going for those walks, you'll work on emptying all of that stuff out that's distracting and plaguing your mind. Sudden revelations, guidance, and awakenings are received from spirit while doing that. Someone goes on their tenth walk and arrives back home with an amazing idea that has filtered through them that was guided by spirit. It turns out to be an answered prayer. Your team can easily work on you when you're not distracted by anything else.

Look at every year as another chapter in the book that is your life. Work with God and your Spirit team by communicating with them regularly on how you would like to see your life mapped out. It doesn't matter if you feel that you're talking to yourself or not hearing them. You are heard and eventually the answer will come to realization for you.

Admitting is the first step to recovery. When you've admitted that the way things are in your life are not jiving with what your soul truly desires now, then the closer you are to progress. You are ready for changes and to have things shaken up a bit. It might seem as if you're off track or at a standstill, but you are on track more than it appears. A standstill feeling is the crossroads point where the inner transformation takes place as you begin to move in the direction towards what you truly love.

CHAPTER FIVE

*Be the Chief Executive
of Your Life*

Who doesn't want positive abundance flowing into their lives? Most everyone desires some level of monetary success to live on the planet comfortably without worry knowing that their bills are paid, with clothes on their back and food on the table. Money is considered evil in some circles, but that is a dramatic statement since money is only as important as the value you place on it. Abundance and success is not only related to money. It can be success in a love relationship or victory in any accomplishment you've succeeded in. This includes one of the most important types of success, which is inner soul triumph

Your soul's life moves in cycles in the same way that your human life moves in phases. These cycles are full of endings and new beginnings. Your day comes to an end when you head off to sleep at whatever time that might be. When you wake up the next day you start a new beginning. Look at this new beginning as if it is a new page within the chapter of the book you're writing that is your life. Twenty-four more hours are put into your next day's bank account. You are the manager of your soul's existence and all choices you decide to make that day. Direct each day in the manner that you would like it to go. Take control of this page within the chapter of your book and write the words that you want to see happen.

When you begin each day with the intention that it will be full of good, then this is far more effective than beginning your day with worry, anger, sadness, or any other negative emotion. The state of mind you choose to begin your day in is what will dictate how your day will go. Wake up each day with the objective that you will feel good. If you're heading to your job, then head into work experiencing greatness! Even if you're not a big fan of your job, it is far more effective energy having a positive mindset and making the most of it rather than shuffling in miserable.

Having a positive mindset is what brightens up your day and those around you. It is also what brings more of that good stuff into your life because this energy is a magnet bringing something of equal or greater value to you. It's inevitable that there will be roadblocks that drop down in the way on your path. You could run into a toxic person while in your car, at a store, on the sidewalk, or at work. When that happens, you will deal with it like an efficient executive since you are the CEO of your life. Allow those moments that ruin your great day to evaporate. Mentally scoop it up with your hand and toss it out like you're pitching a softball as far as it can go. Ask the Archangel Michael to protect and shield you from harsh toxic energies when you begin each day.

Self Fulfilling Prophecies

Everyone wants to feel good each day of their life. Concern settles in when life is not going according to the way you dream or desire. You worry that the things you want will never happen or that you're going to be perpetually stuck. Life is always moving, shifting, and changing. Nothing stays permanently the same. Look at the decisions or the non-action choices you're making or have made that are a result of you feeling stuck. If you get up every morning to spend your day surfing the Internet up until lunchtime, then how will anything change in your life? That's an example of how non-action won't bring you the results you crave. I've heard many cases where someone asks for help in prayer, but nothing comes. What are you doing to help it along? Do you pray and then go back to watching videos, scrolling social media or any other time waster?

There are moments when non-action is an

action in itself. Sometimes you're guided to not make any decisions until the coast is clear or Divine timing has taken place. This is about making no choices that positively contribute to a change happening in your life.

Worry is a fear-based emotion generated from your ego, but it is also part of the natural human experience in order to master it. It is an emotion that creates a block between you and what you crave. It is a normal reaction to feel fear that something is not going the way you hoped. Concern comes about when something isn't going your way or when you're about to make a big change in your life. When this happens, call on your Spirit team and ask them to help give you faith, strength, support, and direction. Ask them to give you confidence and clarity to notice when to take action and to be pushed to do so.

From the angels perspective there is nothing to be concerned about. They see that all will always be well in the end when you have them in your corner. It might feel as if it's impossible not to worry about a situation while you're moving through a specific experience, but when you worry, then you create a self-fulfilling prophecy that brings more obstacles into your life that will add even more anxiety. Thoughts produce things and can magnify a situation by bringing similar situations that are equal to the emotion you're experiencing.

A common phrase I've heard others say is, "Why do bad things keep happening to me?" When you worry about one thing, then this brings about other similar things. When you feel uneasiness about anything at all, then call upon your Spirit team and request that they ease your heart and mind of this worry. Understand the concept that in the bigger picture worry never lasts since situations never last. There are peaks and valleys as well as highs and lows in your life. Eventually your soul will travel back home upon your human death and then the worry is suddenly irrelevant and non-existent.

When experiencing fearfulness, not only is it effective to ask for help, but also work on changing the tone and overall essence of your emotions and thoughts to that of love. This is thinking or saying something like, "All will be well in the end. I know this without a doubt. None of this matters and this too shall pass."

When you lose your job, then the emotions experienced will vary from one person to another. Some will understandably worry about how they will pay their bills, while others will adopt a newfound amazing positive energy out of the job loss. They will see it as a blessing in disguise since deep down they were terribly unhappy at this job to begin with. It was soul crushing and sucking out their life force. When the job was taken away out of nowhere, then their soul eventually experiences freedom. You are now free to start a new chapter in your life wherever you choose. You may still wrestle with the fear of the unknown in that situation. Bills need to be paid to survive so that's an understandable worry. Make a Divine request for a strengthening in faith and to be guided to a brighter situation that will ensure you are physically taken care of financially.

If you've been unhappy at your job, then look for work that will excite you and bring out your passionate side. When something is lost, something else is gained. In order to bring in a new and better situation, the universe will abruptly remove something to make room for what's to come. At first your ego will look at it in panic, while your higher self will see the potential that can come out of it.

This is the same with love relationships. When you lose someone who meant the world to you because that person decided they were no longer interested, or the connection has run its course, then you open the door to allowing someone in who is more aligned with you, your values, and who you are.

In my past work life, I've accepted job offers where I was making less than what I made in prior jobs, but in the end the money multiplied over time to the point where I was making double what I had ever made before. The reason I accepted a job that was little pay was because I eagerly wanted to do that particular work for various reasons, including the knowledge I would gain from the experience. The money came in effortlessly and in bigger ways than it had ever done. This was because my vibration was high. I looked at the job with joy, love, and excitement. I wanted to be doing that kind of work. I would have done it for free. It wasn't about the money and therefore the money came rolling in as a result. Sometimes there is a risk, but I was perfectly content with that chance and the rest came in naturally. When you move through a transition and into a new chapter, then be open to receiving that change in the right spirit!

Noble Service

Focusing on service is a great way to raise your vibration and get the positive energy flowing in your life. It adjusts your focus into helping others instead of being hyper focused on you and how you're feeling at any given moment. When you're focused on yourself, then you're fixated on pleasing your ego. When you're experiencing worry, stress, or anxiety, then adjust your attention in the direction of how you can help someone else in need. It not only alleviates any negative emotions experienced, but it uplifts you to be able to help someone else. This raises your vibration, which then attracts more positive circumstances to you. Suddenly the worries you previously had will evaporate out of your aura and into the universe.

Having a connection with your Spirit team enables you to be able to help others in a positive way. When you're feeling out of sorts or unfocused, then reach out to others to see how you can assist them. This will help raise your vibration to a place of joy and contentment. You'll be on cloud nine when you are able to be of service and help someone out that truly needs it. At the same time be alert to not be taken advantage of by others due to your kindness. You've got to be sensitively sharp and on the psychic ball to see through the dangers of someone taking advantage of you.

This is an egotistical world with a grandiose sense of entitlement, which is a negative side effect to the rise of technology and social media giving everyone a voice. There is a fine line one walks between believing you deserve something to carrying an arrogant air of privilege. If you do not merge into that middle ground mindset, then you'll get walked all over by everyone else.

Society, technology, your peers, the media and the Internet have trained human kind to display a self-absorbed aura. There are good selfless souls threaded around the world to counteract this attitude by being of service. This is not only to help others, but also to show that in the end good deeds prevail. No one warms up to a self-entitled brat, but instead they grow more distant to human kind. Direct your efforts into showing compassion and helping those in need or those who could use a friend and listening ear. This carries over to all aspects of your life.

Working For You

One awesome trait to successful self-employment requires that you be self-disciplined. You take your job seriously as if it were any other job. Instead of answering to someone else, you must answer to yourself. This is a good and bad thing depending on the dynamic. Who doesn't want to turn their hobby into a lucrative enterprise? One of the steps in doing that is to keep your side day job while you work at your hobby. If it truly is your hobby, then it won't feel like a drag to dive into it during off hours. This is another reason guides on the Other Side tend to insist on everyone taking care of themselves on all levels. This way you don't experience early burn out. You have more energy and stamina to do both the regular income-making job, while you work at growing your side hobby business. Taking care of yourself also gives you stronger psychic channels to pick up on the wisdom required.

Don't quit your day job until you know for sure that you are consistently making enough to survive with the incoming money from your hobby. Ask your Spirit team to work with you full time in building your side business into full time work. The Archangels to call on for Heavenly assistance with this are Archangel Gabriel *(motivation manager)*, Archangel Nathaniel *(life purpose work)*, Archangel Michael *(eradicate fear)*, and Archangel Ariel *(abundance and supplies)*.

Know that it may take some time before you are able to quit your regular day job. It could take years, but if you believe it in enough and enjoy what you do, then eventually results will be forthcoming. It also won't feel like work doing what you love on the side. Building a business is like climbing a mountain until you reach the top. It will be a struggle at times, but it is a challenge that you can overcome with an endless reservoir of persistence, dedication, faith, confidence, and passion. This same mindset is the way you rule your life. In a sense, all souls are self-employed at heart. You manage you, your life, relationships, and your entire surroundings with the same commitment and enthusiasm you would as if it we're your own business. You are the chief executive of your life.

Dealing With Life's Setbacks

Many have expressed frustration due to working so hard and contributing so much, yet they feel there isn't enough return or pay off. Maybe you're not being rewarded or compensated at all. While the work itself is its own reward, you live in a world that requires monetary compensation for basic necessities in order to survive. Have patience and keep on trucking forward. A winner perseveres regardless of setbacks, rejections, or delays. Heaven is aware of what you've been doing and they want to see you be at a place where you're at peace. Know that they cannot wave a magic wand and the monetary success you desire comes flying into your lap. They cannot force your next love partner to knock on your front door. They do what they can from where they are to help make things happen for you as long as it's aligned with your higher self's path and not ego filled desires.

They give you clues and signs while attempting to communicate with you on what you can do to help make it happen along quicker through action steps required on your part. When you are in tune, then you are in harmony to the guidance and steps your Spirit team is filtering through you to assist you along your life's path and in conquering your dreams. Keep in mind they are also wrestling with the free will choices of those who can help you attain success.

Roadblocks can be something like you desire a love partner and your team has one in mind. The issue is that both you and this potential partner are not paying attention to your Guide and Angel. Instead you are both ruling through free will choice. One or the both of you might not be following the guidance you're being given. There is a gradual progression upwards towards your dreams as you move through life following the guidance your Spirit team is aiming you towards.

If you are an awesome and wonderful hardworking soul, then avoid allowing negativity to enter your field. Stay focused on what you need to do and be anchored by faith and passion. Circumstances may be dormant, but nothing relatively bad is happening to you, yet you feel stuck beyond comprehension. Look at how far you've come and the progress you've made, rather than why the things you desire have not shown up yet.

Heaven and the angels save you in a myriad of ways that sometimes might seem pretty small at the time, but in hindsight appear fated.

Rock singer Alanis Morissette has one of the bestselling albums of all time called, *Jagged Little Pill*. The album came out about a week after her 21st birthday in 1995. Two years before that she was in a different situation. She was nineteen years old and made a big move to Los Angeles when she immediately ran into some trouble. She was heading home carrying two bags with her. One of the bags had her money in it and the other bag had the lyrics to her not yet recorded album for *Jagged Little Pill.*

A thief was following her and came at her with a gun. She felt enormous panic and fear praying that this person would not take the bag that had her *Jagged Little Pill* lyrics. Guess which bag he took?

He took the bag with her money and not the bag that had her lyrics for *Jagged Little Pill,* an album that was bought by nearly almost everyone on the planet when it came out. It ended up selling over 33 million copies. It's been on numerous top bestselling lists. At press time of this book, it is the 13th highest selling album in history. What if the thief had taken her work instead of the money? There was a reason he was prompted to take the money instead of the art. At that time, she was broke and had not become a financially successful artist yet. The money taken was all of her funds. It was interesting that she was relieved that the money was stolen and not the lyrics.

As a creative artist, I understand how the art can overtake a financial situation. I was working on my computer when out of a clumsy reflex I smacked my tea, which fell onto the keyboard. Within minutes the computer shut down and did not turn back on. My heart raced with panic. This was not because I would have to shelve out money for another computer, but because I had spent the week producing so much writing work that I worried it was gone for good. There is no way I could repeat it word for word. I hadn't yet transferred the work out onto a flash drive for back up as I do pretty regularly. This is not the same as being robbed, but the point was that the money was less of an issue over losing my work. Luckily, the computer was saved as well as my work for a lower fee than anticipated. I also attribute that to asking for immediate Divine assistance and intervention by my team after the accident.

Money is a piece of paper that we apply value to. In the Alanis story she needed money, but it wasn't of importance to her when face to face with the thief. It was the creative art she feared losing. The money came to her later by not craving it on any level. It wasn't something she sought out.

CHAPTER SIX

*Optimistic Visualization,
Getting Enthusiastic and Taking Action*

The power of visualization has been known to create extraordinarily magical results in your life. What assists in contributing to making great things happen are a few central steps: Optimistic Visualization, Paying Attention, and Taking Action.

Optimistic Visualization Foresight

One of the tasks to put into practice towards accomplishing your goals is working on altering your perception into a positive confident mindset. This simple easy reminder is needed for when you stray too far off into negativity that it becomes your

newly adopted personality trait. Positivity equates
to you being a stronger abundance attractor, while
reinforcing your connection with your Spirit team.
This is because positivity and optimism reside in
the higher vibrational energy field. It is the high
vibrational state that allows an effortless connection
with God.

Raising your consciousness simultaneously
raises your vibration giving you a deeper awareness.
This impeccable mindfulness helps in identifying
the subtle cues coming in from the Divine that go
unnoticed within and around you. Those cues are
important because that communication is what is
guiding you towards your purposes that need to be
fulfilled in your lifetime. It is what prompts you to
take notice of when a shift in thinking and feeling
processes on your part is necessary. You were born
able to access Divine communication effortlessly,
but over time blocks rose up in your life that
prevented you from having a crystal clear
connection with God and your Spirit team. One of
the tasks of a spirit guide is to guide you through
life to help it be less friction oriented, than it would
be if they weren't around. They guide you towards
experiences they know will help shape, mold, and
evolve your soul. They want to see the student
snap into soul reality and become blissfully aware of
all that is greater than the limited of the superficial.
This requires your work to tune into them and heed
their guidance.

Having spent my lifetime studying the human
condition to the point of hair splitting, I've noticed
that those who are believers in a higher power and

remain in that state have less of a hard time in life than those that don't believe. This doesn't mean that those who are believers are problem free, but life is not as dramatic without that connection. It's also why gossips and those that love drama seem to have little to no spirit connection while in that state. Their life also seems to be filled with daily negativity and drama.

Another way to achieve your dreams is to put it in your mind that you will obtain what you desire. This is pending that what you desire is not harmful to your well-being or another person's. It will be something beneficial for your higher self's goal and soul's growth. Nothing should stop you from achieving and positively attracting good stuff pending it's not harming yourself or another.

Fears, insecurities, or low self-esteem are abundance success killers. They were born out of the darkness of ego and the human development stage. God and higher evolved beings don't entertain the lower energy, even though there are religious groups that focus on those lower energy elements and then say it's from God. I don't know any God that enjoys the evil and darkness of lower energy. The lower energy is of the Devil and has the intent of sabotaging and criminalizing you. Occasional fears will creep in on you on occasion, but when that's all that plagues your mind daily dominating your thoughts, then it will take over and do its best to destroy your goal. The goal of the Darkness is to stop you from finding the Light. It will do this in ways that convince you that you're unworthy. Avoid allowing negativity to take over and drown you.

Believe you already have what you want. Even when it seems impossible to enter your life, imagine it's a part of your life now. In your mind, close your eyes, and visualize it in motion. Feel it in every crevice of your cells as if it's happening now. Feel the good feelings associated with how you would feel having what you desire. This energy expands and spills into your reality by helping to make it happen from this visualization. This visualization is something that should be done regularly until you have what you desire.

If you desire to buy your own house one day, then begin the visualization of having this house. You can close your eyes at least once a day and envision what this house will look like. You'll visualize its surroundings, the kinds of neighbors that are around you, the location, and everything about it. You'll then visualize yourself living in this house, walking around throughout it, sleeping in your bed in this house, making a meal in the kitchen, the kinds of friends you have visiting this house, or the love partner that is with you in this house, and so on. Notice your feelings and state of mind and how you'll feel while living in this house as this is happening.

You can apply this visualization exercise to whatever you desire, whether it's a love relationship, job, car, or anything you desire. This is pending it is aligned with your higher self's purpose and God's will. The benefits to this visualization exercise are that it programs your mind to move away from the doubts and fears that you'll attract this in. It also assists in getting the positive energy surrounding this visualization towards making it happen.

When you wallow in negative feelings and thoughts that you'll never attract in what you desire, then this creates a separation between yourself and this desire that grows wider and further away from you. When you think good stuff associated with this desire, then it starts to bring the aspiration closer to you through this energy. You're already creating with your thoughts and feelings anyway, so you may as well make it positive oriented.

Using your imagination visually paint the picture of what you desire. Experience feelings associated with confidence and enthusiasm surrounding this visual, as if it is real and here in your life happening now. Avoid allowing doubts or worry to enter your mind as that can negate the process. When you experience negative feelings, then this energy multiplies causing more of that pessimism to come into your vicinity.

Optimistic visualization is about believing that what you want is coming to you with great veracity. Some achieve this by creating a vision board. A vision board or visual scrapbook is cutting out photographs of ideas of what you would like to have in your life. Pick up magazines to find these images or print them off your computer. You can use the vision board for whatever you choose from the kind of house you would like to live in, to the type of love interest you envision having, or for any other desires.

The reason some put a vision board together is

because it helps them focus on what they want without forgetting about it or veering away from it. If they wake up every morning and the first thing they see is the vision board they made, then those images continue to build and seep into that person's consciousness. This is the same as those that have empowering words carved out and hanging around their house. It serves as a reminder so that they don't forget. The world is a busy place and people are distracted and rushing around. You're focused on negative feelings or on mundane practical tasks that need to get done. Soon you find that you've grown stuck in that routine energy. If you have these images and words up around your home, on your computer screen, or in a specific place where you see it regularly, then this triggers the essence, energy, and vision of what you want.

You've had another trying day at work arriving home beat and defeated. The first thing you see when you walk into your place is this board you created reminding you of the things you desire. It uplifts you a bit to see these images. Not everyone will want to have this vision board up on the mantle in their living room where all who come to visit see it. Perhaps it doesn't go with your décor. Find a place where you remember to catch a glimpse of it or have access to it. You can certainly shove it in your closet out of view from visitors, but don't forget it's there. Maybe stick it in a corner in your room or any other place that you know you'll remember having it.

A vision board or motivating words on a mantel are a reminder to stay focused on your purpose and visualize what you want. The images you put on this board are right in front of you. Sometimes pulling the board down and gazing at the images or words at the end of the night or at the start of your day can help uplift you and put a smile on your face reminding you of what you desire. This uplifting feeling raises your vibration back up. What a great way to start each day.

The power of optimistic visualization is immensely helpful in obtaining your desires. Sometimes one can forget what's important when they are bogged down in the practicalities of their everyday life. They forget to daydream and visualize what will make them happy.

Daydreaming includes the dreams you have while sound asleep to the kinds of imaginative visuals you conjure up in your mind during waking hours. If you're someone that has frequent vivid dreams, then one of your dominant psychic senses is Clairvoyance.

Keep a notepad or journal near you to jot down key visuals that are in your dreams. Dreams tend to fade immediately or within minutes to an hour after waking. This is the benefit of writing it down quickly before you forget. Otherwise you'll find you're one of those people who later in the day says, "I had the greatest dream last night, but I can't remember any of it."

You only remember the feeling it gave you. Your subconscious mind is where the greatest psychic input resides because your ego is asleep at that time. It's not getting in your way of receiving heavenly guidance and messages to discredit it.

Souls with an active imagination prone to daydreaming are that much closer to understanding the process of manifestation. A jaded blocked adult might tell a child, "Get your head out of the clouds and quit daydreaming."

This is tragic since the child has a better shot at manifesting their desires over the cynical adult. Daydreaming requires one to be still and allow their thoughts to drift away from what is their current reality. Some daydream in order to escape an unhappy life. It's used as a safety device as they imagine what they wish their life would be like. Daydreaming is an escape in this scenario and used for their protection. If your home life is horrible or abusive, then it's not uncommon for that person to become a daydreamer of a life that is more pleasing to that person.

Daydreaming is also a great way to connect with Heaven and your Spirit team, since your thoughts are relaxed and moving towards what you desire. You're open to receiving psychic hits, messages, and guidance. Daydreaming is typically filled with positive wish-filled thoughts, which raise ones vibration and assists in manifesting good things in that individual's life. Great ideas come to you when you are in a daydream state since your connection to your Guides and Angels is stronger. You're not pushing for Divine information while in a daydream state, so it flows through you naturally.

Get Happy Now
and the Rest Will Follow

Getting positive and optimistic isn't about covering up your negative thoughts with phony positive ones. The positive thoughts and feelings need to be authentic and unforced, otherwise it's just a negativity mask in disguise like hiding a cut behind a Band-Aid. Feel the good energy by partaking in fun healthy activities that you know will raise your vibration. Feeling positive thoughts and feelings authentically is experiencing those vibrations inside you.

Ask for Heavenly intervention and help through prayer, then pay attention to the guidance you're expected to take action on and take that action. You may not receive an answer at the time you're praying, but ask God and your Spirit team to show you signs of what to do. Request that they continuously reveal this answer in a way that you can recognize it.

Divine guidance will usually come to you three times or more. It repeatedly enters your auric field through your psychic clair senses in hopes you'll discover that it's a message. When your psychic senses are strong, then you're more likely to pick up on the messages coming in. Your Spirit team will continue to give you the same signs until you notice it.

Bring in what you desire by allowing it to flow towards you naturally. You're not chasing your dreams in a panic. You're taking productive action steps through methodical movements with love to obtain what you long for. If there's someone you're interested in romantically, then ask them out whether or not you're male or female. Regardless of their answer, don't chase or burden them by staying on top of them relentlessly. When it's the right one, it will flow and merge with you naturally and organically. Placing any kind of demands will push it away. The same goes for work related endeavors or anything you have your eyes set on. The serious relationships I've had over the course of my life all transpired without effort. It came to be when I wasn't looking or longing, but when I was content. When I was frustrated or in a negative mindset, nothing came to pass.

Actress Nicole Kidman once said there was a time when her fantasy life was richer than her reality. She dove into working on back-to-back films because her real life outside of work was less than she originally hoped. Over time this was reversed where her real life became everything she dreamed of with the house, husband, and family. Those particular things may not be of interest to you, but the point was that she escaped into work not realizing these other things outside of that were being moved into position. She worked hard and the rewards she desired eventually one day came.

If you continuously fall into a negative mindset, then be aware of when that happens and mentally tell yourself something like, *"I need to adjust the vibration levels of my thinking."*

Follow that with shifting and raising the negative direction of your thoughts into optimistic ones. When you've been wallowing in negativity, then that can block good stuff from flowing to you. It's easy to fall into despair and frustration when enormous time has passed, and your desires haven't manifested into reality. When you look back on the passing time, it might seem that nothing in your life has changed. You feel stagnant like being indefinitely stuck in the mud. You crave positive change and stimulation, but good stuff ceases to flow in. There isn't anything bad or negative happening in your life, which is a blessing that isn't often appreciated, but there is zero movement with anything at all. You are not where you thought or envisioned you would be five years prior. This can put a damper on your faith as you wonder what you've been doing wrong. When this happens, revert back to faith and prayer to help re-align your soul. This is when you discover that the stagnancy is no accident. Even Jesus was in living in stagnant obscurity for a long period of time before that began to change.

Paying Attention

Pay attention to the guidance and messages that your Spirit team is relaying to you. If you're unclear on what your next step should be, then carve out some time where you can sit quietly in meditation. Meditation helps you pick up on the guidance from spirit coming in. Some have expressed uncertainty on how to meditate or what it is. You move into a slight meditative state as you drift off to sleep at night without realizing it. It dissolves or reduces your waking ego and brings forth your consciousness. The answers come in clearer when you are calm, peaceful, centered, and in a setting that matches those traits. This is one of the many reasons that the angels advise that human souls be outdoors in nature. Nature settings are calming and it relaxes the mind. When the mind is relaxed, then the messages and guidance are picked up on in a clearer way. There is no distraction of the physical material world when you are hanging out in a low crowded nature setting. It takes some measure of discipline, since you need to shut off all noisy distractions such as television, cell phones, and boisterous people.

I've had cases where I sit down and Heaven's messages rush in out of nowhere, but then my phone buzzes near me and I have this urge to reach for it. After a number of times of being easily distracted I finally mumble, "Okay, that's it. This needs to be off."

I turn the phone off or put it in another room where I'm unable to hear it vibrating. My mind moves incredibly fast where I'm seeing and picking up on every nuance. I have to be disciplined about my surroundings when it's time for me to get down to psychic business.

If you have trouble meditating due to not being focused, then create an atmosphere that works for you. This would be one that is set up in a way that easily moves you into a peaceful state. One way to do this is to find a place where there are no obtrusive distractions. Play some soft background music, light a candle, then sit and focus on it. Allow any mindless chatter or distracting energies to evaporate. Sitting or lying down works, but you might find that when you lay down that you drift off to sleep. It is okay if this happens since your Spirit team embeds messages into your consciousness. If clairvoyance is one of your stronger Clairs, then you might get the messages and guidance while dreaming.

If you're new to meditation, then don't worry if you're not receiving anything right away. The first number of times practice meditating without any intention of picking up on your Spirit team's guidance. When you strain to receive messages, then this blocks you from obtaining anything. Sometimes the guidance can come in after you've relaxed in meditation. You might have spent about fifteen minutes in this meditation state where you've cleared your mind and then you get up to continue on with your life. It's not uncommon for there to be a delay before you pick up on the messages. As you're getting ready for bed later on, suddenly the crystal clear Heavenly guidance comes rushing in through one of your Clair channels. You cry out, "That's it! That's the answer."

You're swiftly filled with excitement and optimism, which is another sign that you've received Heavenly guidance, since there are no doubts, worry, or any other negative feeling involved when it's guidance from Heaven.

Divine Guidance Through Action

You may start to fear that Spirit and Heaven are ignoring you or perhaps the non-movement is out of your hands. Consider the possibility that Spirit is diligently working behind the scenes throughout that entire time and have not had much luck getting things moving for you. They have to work with other people's free will choices that go against what is intended to take place. They're also putting up signs, guidance, and messages for you or others to take action on. You or another might be ignoring those action steps, sometimes for years thus no movement happens during that time. They can't reveal the next step until the first action step they've been throwing in front of you is taken. It doesn't matter if that action step takes one month or ten years. The same repetitive action step will keep popping up in front of you for a reason until you notice it and take action on it.

There can be cases where you have been putting in the tireless work and action steps. There is nothing you did wrong to cause your life to feel forever stationary. There could be other factors at play to consider. Some of that might be the maneuvering of the puzzle pieces your Spirit team is attempting to orchestrate to help move things along. There are also the free will choices you or another party is choosing that go against what Spirit is recommending. Spiritual teachings contribute Divinely guided information to help those interested in becoming clearer vessels for God, which simultaneously has a positive effect on your soul's consciousness.

In an earlier chapter I mentioned that it took me seven years to get into the film business. I was sixteen years old when I psychically knew that was going to be my next big move. It wasn't until I turned twenty-three years old when it worked out in my favor. That's seven years of what felt like stagnancy. What did I do during that time? I obtained my first regular job as a teenager at the record store chain when those existed. I simultaneously studied up on the creative side of the film business, I read and wrote in journals, I experienced life, perfected my resume, made lists of entertainment production companies and contacted them. My general disposition was that I was going to get in and nothing was going to stop me. I said, "I will never stop trying to get in. I will keep doing that until I'm eighty, I don't care."

I had the occasional doubt or frustration with, "This is ridiculous. When is it going to happen?"

Those negative moments were rare, because that wasn't my general disposition. 95% of the time I was focused on getting in with excitement. I kept working hard to achieve it, then by the force of a miracle from above I got in. What are the odds that a movie star is going to hire some young punk kid with no experience? There was regular praying and taking action steps on my part until one day I received that surprise call back.

In fact, when the call came in I was so stunned that it took me an hour to center myself before calling back. It seemed too good to be true that I went into this hazy state of shock not believing it.

The point of sharing that tidbit of a story was that I was no one in particular, without any experience, but myself to sell. This means that anybody has the capability of doing it if they have passion, persistence, hard work, and a great attitude.

After talking to me, the production company discovered that underneath that punk rebellious aura there was as one of them put it, "....a super high intellect that dominated..." the bosses. This was considered a strength and asset to the company. Use who you are, your personality, and those parts of you to showcase to the world. People love authenticity and originality. Those that make big decisions such as hiring gravitate towards someone different than the norm.

Act and follow the guidance that your Spirit team has relayed to you. Sitting on your couch all day waiting for a blessing to ring your doorbell is highly unlikely to happen. You meet your Spirit team half way by asking them what steps you need to take next. Perhaps the message you receive is to re-send out your resume to a place you already sent it to, but received no response originally. Now your team is asking you to forget about all that and send it again. You send out your resume to the same place as your team requested, only this time you get a response asking you to come in for an interview or meeting.

Sometimes the messages and guidance might seem insignificant or trivial. I've relayed messages and guidance from my team asking me to discuss these basic steps of meditation and hammer home the nature setting again. That seems trivial initially, but as I illustrated it's for good reason that can help benefit your life. Rushing around stressed out wondering when your life will change is not going to allow you to pick up on Heaven's messages, which are delivered to assist in enhancing your life.

It is a tough process achieving what you've always wanted to do, but you can do it! Take it one step at a time and eventually you will master it. When it's something you really want to do, then there's nothing you cannot accomplish. It's that passion, drive, and persistence that is your winning card. It doesn't feel like a chore when it's something you love. You want to learn about the processes and different avenues you can take to reach that goal.

What you can do before you do anything is change your thoughts and get positive. Look at the bright side of what you have in your life today. Take a second and allow the good stuff to flush through you now. Visualize what you desire to see in your life, get optimistic and excited about it, ask for help from above, and then take action and work hard to achieve it.

CHAPTER SEVEN

Partake in Pleasing Work

Some believe that if you're given a gift, a particular talent, or a divinely inspired idea, then you should give it away without charging money for it. There's the romanticized old view of the starving artist pining away in a tin can, which is absurdly unrealistic. In today's age, unless you were born into money or you're living off a large trust fund, then if you want to survive you'll need to work to make money. You have to charge for your gifts and services, not out of greed, but so you can pay for rent, food, and clothing. When those basic necessities are taken care of, then you're able to focus on what you love without worry or concern of survival.

If you gave everything away for free, then you couldn't survive. You would have to find a super uncreative full time job on the side to pay your bills, but that could sap your creative energy and life force anyway.

There was a time when people would barter and do a trade with someone, but now necessities cost money. This is why spiritual teachers charge. The only spiritual teachers that don't charge are those who work in a church, but those are non-profit companies where they are receiving donations from members of the congregation to stay afloat. If they didn't receive donations, then they would close up and many of them have. That money goes into their paychecks and the upkeep of the church, so even they are charging essentially.

There are a great many talented healers and artists contributing positive work and efforts towards humanity and their life purpose, but sadly many of them are stuck in regular day jobs that suck up their time and energy. This makes it challenging to pursue their true passion and make a decent living out of it. What makes that feeling worse is that an enormous amount of these day jobs lower their morale. This is because those jobs are bathed in toxic energy in one person or more around them that are disconnected from spirit and the bigger universal picture. If that's not the case and all are a pleasure to be around, then the lowered morale can come from your lengthy commute to the job, or because the job is not your passion. That alone can be the reason for the lowered morale. As a sensitive this can be exceptionally taxing on your well-being system, but this is tiring on anyone regardless if they are psychically in tune or not. Being aware of what's greater than your physical body makes it more depressing to be in Earthly set ups that bring you permanently down.

If you're in this kind of a situation, then you are aware that a high percentage of your time is connected to this day job on some level even when you're not at work. This can stall a talented person from working towards what they want to do with their life in the long run. They soon give up and lose faith believing that the Universe is working against them and that they're just not as lucky in the way that others are. Don't give up on the account of someone else. It can be tough at times, but you have to keep going and fighting to do what your soul agreed to do.

One guy informed me that when he's not at work he's sometimes having dreams at night that involves his place of employment or about his colleagues. It didn't start off that way, but when the feeling of wanting to do what he loved grew, then his hatred for his day job grew, which started to manifest into his dreams. This day job became embedded deeply into his consciousness. When you're asleep and having dreams about your job, then that's a problem. Your energy is too mired and infiltrated into something that doesn't mean that much to you in the end. You're not at work and you're still thinking about it! It's not even a job he likes all that much, but he's always there which means there isn't enough balance of personal and professional time. Most of his days are spent at his job the way most do. This is not entirely his fault as that's the way the current break-your-back mentality mindset of human physical life is at this time.

Find meaningful work at a place that excites you. Consider the steps you can take today to change this whether that is through job hunting or home and apartment hunting. Imagine how many years you can endure in your current state before your spirit is permanently crushed. Working with a weaker boss can add more frustration and stress.

A fearful boss that lacks in confidence will ask, "How did this happen?"

A confident assertive fearless boss asks, "How do we fix this?"

This is because the stronger boss is interested in moving things forward. The weaker boss asks how something happened to stall forward movement and to place blame, which doesn't improve momentum or morale.

"How do we fix this?" is someone looking to keep things going. They have the desire to get others to think outside the box and provide solutions to quickly remedy an issue without wasting any additional time on it. This is the same thought process to have in all of your dealings in life from your daily choices, to your love and friendship connections.

Most jobs require you to be in the office full time, which is currently set to five days a week – eight hours a day. This varies depending on what city or country you reside in. The time you devote to your job doesn't include the getting ready for work, and driving to and from your place of employment, or your mid-day hour break, which I've discovered many rarely take.

This is also connected to the break your back work mentality that egotistical human beings designed. They had no concept of balance when they set it up that way. No one is happy about it, and bosses and superiors are unaware of it or don't care. Part of that is because they choose their own hours where they may work from home for a few hours before going into the office, or they take their time going in. They receive a larger compensation for the work. When you get paid super well, then you're more gung ho about your job. This is up to a point since those who have larger dreams of doing work they love will do it for free if they had all the time and energy in the world.

Increase Faith To Attract

In the films *Passengers* and *Cast Away*, both show one person functioning alone for a long period of time, and eventually starting to go a little mad due to not having another person to engage with at some point.

If someone showed up on Earth to find no other people, then he wouldn't know what he was missing. Because there is no material distraction, he would be more in tune to the Heavens unable to hear anything else. This is how human beings progressed in the beginning of civilization. They paid attention to the Heavens and their Divine senses to guide them on how to naturally progress.

Eventually as progression took place, so did material and physical drive. This expanded and exploded to the point of never ending distractions. The more this chaos rose up, the less Divinely connected human beings became. There is no way to escape that and not be aware that it's happening, even if you live in the middle of nowhere. While you might be more connected to Spirit in those areas, you lose the connection when you turn your television on, you surf the internet, you read media stories, or you hop on your phone. Now you are no longer spiritually connected. You might be connected to one another through technological devices, but in a distant loveless way. You are not connected to God through those forms.

The entire planet is unsettled and distracted, which makes it near impossible to sense the Divine energy that way. Your subconscious is aware of it, even if you're not paying attention to it in the present moment. However, if you're a highly spiritually connected being, then you're versed and readily able to move in and out of the Spirit connection whenever it calls for it.

Your soul's life force dies little by little living a life you're unhappy with. Perhaps you feel emotionally dead as if you don't have much else to give anymore. You've asked for help for years, and became doubtful that it will ever happen at this point. You're waiting, hoping, praying, and taking action for years wondering if a miracle and blessings will reveal itself to you. It can make you doubt, lose faith, and question if there is a God. It sounds like a roller coaster ride of voices competing with one another from your ego to your angels, to your ego, to your angels.

It is not uncommon to feel disconnected from other people when your consciousness is raised. Suddenly human life appears trivial and superficial. You begin to isolate as a result of not feeling like you can connect with people that understand or can relate to you. Do an inventory check of how the months and years to date have gone in your life. Examine your triumphs, your sorrows, your successes, and your challenges. Look at what was lost and what was gained. You'd be surprised to find the hidden blessings you never thought much of until you look back on it. When things are going swimmingly, people don't often notice it as much as they do when things are going horribly wrong. One can take it for granted until you take a moment to ponder on it.

"Okay my rent gets paid every month, my health is great, and I have a working car that gets me to work."

Look forward to the coming time up ahead with promise and hope. Have faith and believe that it will get better by accepting nothing less than that mindset.

Success comes and goes the way fame comes and goes. One of the best dreams to come true is being able to turn your love and hobby into a financially lucrative career. You are closer than someone else might be because you understand the concept of manifestation and asking for what you want. If you're stressed out at your job regularly, is the job really worth it? Make wise choices in your life that do not result in leaving you in a bind where you're perpetually unhappy. Take a job for less pay, live beneath your means, until you find the work that makes you feel bliss again.

Looking to the future with optimism you might sometimes find you've been chasing rainbows that evaporate as quickly as the champagne fizzles in your glass. You need not search long and hard for some measure of magic to reveal itself since it's always resided within you. You are loved even when you doubt it, avoid it, shun it and do everything in your power to deny it. When you reach that threshold of completing your Earthly run, the only thing you take with you is love. If you gain anything while here, then remember to love more, give more, and have compassion no matter how unpopular it is. Only then can you truly discover that magic you secretly desire.

CHAPTER EIGHT

You Are Worthy and Deserving of Blessings

It takes a warrior like effort to not allow anything to kill off your life force and prevent you from working on your passion and life purpose. There are a great many rags to riches stories that included people that were once struggling and wondering if they'd ever break free from their self-imprisoned life, but they kept working hard on what they desired on the side during their down time. Eventually, they transitioned out of that and into what they love.

Keep forging on ahead fearlessly and making a personal pact to contribute a little bit of what you love towards your lifelong goals each day for a minimum of thirty minutes to an hour. Whether that hour is used to read and research up on your areas of interest, or to devote positive action steps towards what will ultimately be your life purpose income, such as creating a website, a social media page, postcards, etc. Putting in a tiny bit of time is better than putting in no time.

Become an independent, confident, and self-sufficient self-starter that manages your life with enthusiasm and finesse. It's a world of workaholics plugging away at meaningless tasks that usually amount to a great deal of nothing in the end. This carries off into all aspects of your life, but is primarily beneficial for those in leadership or supervising positions.

When spreading yourself too thin, you want to ensure to be extra careful about what you're putting into your body. You might complain you're too tired or don't have enough time or energy to contribute up to an hour a day into what could potentially be your full-time job. This is a dilemma and a block for you, but if this is work you truly love, then it doesn't feel like work. It's something you enjoy doing, so working on it is rarely a problem. When someone cheerfully wants to do something, then they will do it no matter how tired they are. In fact, putting in work on your passion and love gives you a positive lift, a boost, and raises your vibration. All of which are ingredients in that recipe for attracting in positive circumstances, more energy, and abundance.

Raising your vibration is a crucial element in giving you greater energy and a brighter mood.

This encourages you to make the time to contribute towards what you love. After a long laborious and tedious day at work at your day job, you may be sapped of life force energy to keep going with your passion. When you have more continuous energy, then that's energy to help push you to contribute towards work that you love, such as your life purpose passion work during those moments when you're not at your day job.

The reason you might be exhausted at the end of each day is not always because work is so tough at your day job, but it's because this job does not excite you on any level. When you experience excitement, then the feel good chemical dopamine is released into your system naturally. When you despise what you do, then this depletes the dopamine chemical, which sucks the life force energy right out of you making you feel tired. You then reach out for artificial substances to create the feelings you need.

When I'm doing what I love, then the energy keeps going beyond twelve hours where I don't want to stop. It's a perpetual rushed excited high, because I'm doing what I love that it doesn't feel like work. It's fun and I'm getting paid for it too! On top of that I'm being extra careful with what I put into my body and system. You know that if you have a glass of wine or a beer in the middle of the day, then you're unlikely to put in any work into what you love. Do the work first, complete it, and then celebrate with your beer. Keeping your energy high and motivated on those days that you want to work on your life purpose requires taking care of all aspects of your body, mind, and soul. When you believe that great things will happen for you, then great things will happen! The ingredients in this recipe include having a positive attitude, strong faith, asking for help in prayer, and taking action. Like the Journey song title says, "Don't stop believing."

For some successful people, there will come that point when the floodgates of blessings and abundance open and it soars wonderfully into your world. Some personalities will allow the darkness of ego to rise convincing you to panic, fear, and worry that it's a fluke and will be taken away from you soon enough. Some form of worry could be considered understandable, but don't let it consume and drown you. Quickly move away from that way of thinking and receive the blessings with a positive spirit.

Whenever I started a new film production for the studios, people were unaware that I had the occasional minor fear briefly in the beginning years. I would worry the first few days that I might get fired. I would go into a serious meditation exercise the night before my first day on the job and be prepared to dive on in and hit the ground running. The minor fear or worry was so miniscule though that it didn't dominate, but was rather a fleeting thought that peeked its face in, then blew away just as quickly. After the first number of days on the gig the fears would subside, as I'd fall into the comfortable rhythm and groove of the job. Employers would later comment they were surprised to hear that I'd have doubts in the beginning because it never showed. It would pop in for thirty seconds, then pop right out as I'd realign, let it go, and just do the best job I can do.

It's a wonderful and awesome thing when circumstances start flowing positively. You think, "Wow, I can't believe how great this is. I hope it doesn't go away and I don't lose it."

Don't doubt, just accept, and enjoy the wave of excitement and optimism. Allow any roadblocks in your life to fall away as you move into smooth calm waters up ahead.

Get optimistic, have faith, and trust in God and your Spirit team. When you're worried about something, then ask and pray for intervention to remove those worries. Make this prayer request daily if the worry continues. Don't give up or try to do it yourself, but turn your worries into prayer, since that's what can help lift the burdens that negative thoughts and feelings can produce.

Prayer is intended to help you move away from worry and fear. You invalidate a prayer when you continue to worry afterwards. The worry tells Spirit that you don't trust their intervention and assistance and so you will continue to worry as a backup plan in case God doesn't come through. When you receive repeated nudges after the prayer to take action on something, then take action.

When circumstances become too great, then take some time out in quiet meditation or contemplation. Create a sanctuary ambiance at home or in your room. Disconnect from people and technology for several hours or even the day, and spend that time conversing with God, a higher power, and the universe. Go on a day or weekend trip with a positive friend or by yourself if you find that more beneficial.

Let go of feelings of resentment and jealousy about other people who seem to be more successful than you are at this point. This success may be in career, love, or life in general. You want to avoid falling into that kind of envy energy because that will ensure you stay single or will never be successful. It's understandable to a point that you are feeling frustrated because you are just as deserving of a good life as anyone else. Resentment builds and overpowers you and crushes your soul in the process.

The flipside is if you are financially successful, then don't feel guilty about making money in general, or making more money than others. Money is energy, so when you're being paid for services you provide, then that is an exchange of energy. Feel no guilt about making money or how you choose to spend it. You are worthy of making money for any work you do. Don't apologize for being blessed.

Avoid resentment, jealousy, worry, or fear associated with money. Visualize the awesome circumstances you'd be able to partake in due to making enough money. Imagine how many people's lives you'd be able to change and help positively.

Your imagination is a powerful divine instrument of God so use it to your advantage. You're already spending the day thinking, perhaps thinking about useless chores and tasks, but how about thinking about something good. Pay attention to those ideas that enter your mind. A great deal of it is coming from above. Look at the great music, books, art, and movies over the course of history alone that started out with one person's idea and rapidly expanded to the point where there is a 600-man crew filming it into a visual story. It's awesome what people have been able to create over Earth's progression.

The angels don't want to see someone destined for greatness working in a day job that kills off their life force. They are not keeping you down and nor are they keeping you there to punish you. There could be various reasons as to why you're still there that is beyond your control. They could be working diligently behind the scenes with aligning circumstances that work in your favor to get you to work full time in your self-employed business.

Release any vows of poverty you might have made in a past life, regardless if you believe in past lives or not. It won't hurt you to verbally say, "I release all vows of poverty I might have made in this life or any previous ones, in all directions of time."

There are some circumstances, which cannot practically be understood by the human mind. Navigate through life with an open and awakened mind and consciousness over what is unseen.

Have no fear or doubts in believing in Heaven, God, Jesus, and your Spirit team. Believe that you are watched over and are not being ignored, even on those days when you just want to throw in the towel and permanently give up. Don't give up because there is a reason you are here. Spirit can see the good up ahead even when you feel like this is it.

The world spins around, circumstances change, friendships come and go, some stay, some leave, people pass on, life goes on for the soul. Study and read up on success stories that you can do it! Don't feel resentment or jealousy over someone else's work, but feel inspired and motivated by it instead. It's to help you feel those things so that you can believe that yes you can do it too.

When one thinks of success they automatically equate it to money, but success is not always financial or monetary. The utmost form of success is how evolved your soul develops in one lifetime. Since this is the true measure of Spirit's view of success, then you should thrive to push the billionaire mark. Rise above the world around you and dive deep into the depths of possibilities by working to expand your mind and consciousness. Seek out the vast reservoirs of wisdom, knowledge, and intelligence that the Universe holds. Take that by the reigns and soar full speed ahead today. Make some great things happen in your life now.

Manifesting

One of the keys to manifesting is having an unwavering passion for a desire. You can have anything you want and can cause anything to happen when you have unbending passion for it. This is where you feel this passion for your desire all over you, within you, and around you. You feel and know it in your mind. You feel and know it in your heart. You feel and know it all throughout your body and soul. You know without a doubt that it will happen and that it is here now. It's allowing this feeling to build to the intensity of an erupting volcano. You feel this desire continue to rise with positive excitement from within. There are no negative feelings associated with this passionate feeling. You visually see what you want happening in reality with great optimism.

If you are having a passion for obtaining something, but you have doubts circling that, then the doubts will overpower the desire and you will receive the doubts instead of the desire. Experience inner peace and uplifting joy that you're living this vision as if it is real time. It is seeing this vision as if it is here and happening now. Hold this intention daily and avoid negative thoughts from taking over. It is not enough to visualize something you want, but to also take action steps to get there. When you have a passion for something, you naturally want to dive into that passion. Having passion is a joyous feeling. It's the key to manifesting positively.

Once this is complete, then the difficult step is to then let it go. It's to release this vision and desire of what you want to your higher self, God, or your Spirit team. It's completely letting go of this desire and not caring about it. It's releasing and surrendering it to the higher power. The reason this is a challenging step is because most people find it difficult to let go of something they really want. They fixate on it heavily never letting the desire go. This then moves into obsessive doubts and concerns that it will never happen. However, if this last step is not followed, and you do not let this desire go and release it, then the manifestation connection is not fully made. It may push the outcome further away from you. This gives you an idea as to why your desire is not coming to fruition. You must let it go and move onto the next manifestation. Do not concern yourself with the how or when a manifestation will occur as this will block it. If you obsess over a desire, then you will block it from manifesting. Instead, you will receive negative manifestations or you'll find that you're in a stagnant position where there is no movement at all.

I've always been manifesting, as everyone is manifesting whether they're aware of it or not. I've been manifesting since I was a teenager through this process I describe. One of the many secrets was by stepping into my Divine power as a fearless confident spirit. I had passion and a steady, calm, euphoric positive energy surrounding what I wanted. I use the word passion to describe this process. If you don't have passion for something, then it will show. It doesn't matter what your expertise is or what kind of degree you have. None of that matters because if you have no passion for what you're doing, then that will come through. You need to passionately want it, but then let go of knowing, how, or when it will happen.

When I first started out in the entertainment business, I had no skills or experience to warrant getting a job in that industry. All I had to sell them with was my personality, drive and passion. I walked in there and conveyed how much I wanted it and how right I was for the gig. There was no acting needed, because I genuinely wanted it with incredible veracity. I went after every job position with this same passion and I was hired. This same manifestation process was the same process for how I became an author. I knew I was going to do it. I clairvoyantly saw it up ahead.

I've been following my own Spirit team's guidance, messages, and steps relayed to me from as far back as a teenager. This equivalent method was also the case with all of the relationships I was involved in. I knew without a doubt that I would be with a particular person. Granted, I'm sure in hindsight, I might have paid bigger attention to the red flags presented, but the point is to be careful what you wish for. If the wish is felt with great positive veracity, passion, and steadfast intensity, then you just might get it. This includes what you don't want. If you are intensely worried about something, then you are giving that attention energy you don't want to be feeding it with. It will end up expanding and bringing on more of that comparable energy into your life.

CHAPTER NINE

Awaken Your Creative Spirit

When you cannot seem to shake the uncomfortable rut of negative feelings plaguing and dominating your life, then dive into a creative project or hobby. Creative pursuits raise your soul's energy vibration and lift the passion quotient within you. When you immerse yourself in a creative hobby, then this opens up your heart, enhances your soul, and brings more joy into your life. Since immersing oneself raises your vibration, this attracts in good stuff and optimistic feelings to you outside of the creative hobby. If you do not have any creative interests, then consider looking at obtaining one. Creative interests can be anything from picking up a paint-by-number set, to training yourself to play a musical instrument, to pottery making to taking an acting class. There are endless ways to awaken the creative part of you.

Diving into creativity is a great way to shake yourself out of any funk you experience. It helps you navigate through the treacherous waters of human life. It assists you in finding innovative ways to solutions, which can carry over to other aspects of your life from the business arena to love relationships. It helps you to think outside of the box and showcase your originality because everything you're doing while being creative is solely you. It pulls out the deepest parts of your soul. A photographer is being creative by taking pictures. They might spend hours taking a variety of photos of different flowers in a garden. By doing this they see the beauty around them, which is often overlooked. These creative gifts come out of you and mirror what you have within. Your true nature is revealed back to you as a result.

Your soul is magnificently wonderful and loved by God and the universe beyond measure and comprehension. How awesome is that to be unconditionally loved no matter how you're feeling? All human souls desire to be loved and will seek it out in friendships, family members, colleagues and lovers. This is with the hope that these other souls will give you that all-encompassing love, but always fall short in some people's eyes. The love exists within you to begin with and can be conjured up naturally. This is God's love for you.

Creativity is a great reminder of who your soul truly is. It brings this love back out of you. Creativity cures any boredom or lulls in your day while helping you to express yourself in positive ways. When someone is bored they tend to reach for an addiction. They might log online, surf the Internet pointlessly, visit a social media site, or log on to a phone app for human contact and stimulation that ceases to exist in their physical reality. You feel even more lonely and bored after hours of being unproductive. This becomes a bigger problem when you discover that this is how you spend every second of your day. If you didn't have that one step to check your social media page throughout the day, then you fear you might lose out on life. I've had friend's say, "Okay I've been on [social media] too much lately. I need to take a step back."

They're going crazy inside realizing it's not fulfilling anything positive for them. This is more about someone that spends each day for months surfing the internet out of lethargy while accomplishing nothing.

Artistic creative souls also have a higher attraction to abusing addictions and toxic substances. The same goes for those who are sensitive or psychically connected. If you are a sensitive, psychically connected, artistic, and creative, then the odds of you succumbing to a toxic vice or addiction runs higher than if you are one or the other. In many cases, having all of these traits go hand in hand with the super connected.

If you're a creative soul that regularly dives into artistic pursuits, then it's likely you have deeper psychic gifts than the average person. You may be aware of it or you are about to begin realizing the connection between both. When an artist doesn't create for long periods of time, then it can feel like you're running out of air. Creative inspiration is heavenly guided and influenced by Spirit. Your Spirit team plays a hand in it as well as the Archangel Gabriel, who joins the creative soul being to assist in the inspiration and motivation process. Archangel Gabriel is the hierarchy angel that oversees all creative souls who choose to turn their gifts into a lifelong hobby or career.

Artists are sensitive and can access and channel this inspiration often without knowing it. Channeling comes naturally to them, regardless if they are a believer in something outside of themselves or not.

If you fit this description, know that you are immensely gifted rather than cursed. The curse is when you feel unable to control the access of information or creativity that pours into you. This ends up propelling you to reach for toxic substances that might be considered an addiction.

Part of your soul's growth is to gain control and master your ego. This may take a lifetime depending on one's individual journey. You can become a master at being disciplined and yet you still find yourself tumbling down the rabbit hole every once in awhile. When that happens, call on Heaven for support. Don't beat yourself up over it. I have been a lifelong addict, but others claim or protest to view me as being completely together, strong, and independent. It doesn't matter, because the addiction gene runs right through the human development part of my soul. It's something I wrestle with no matter how connected I am. I do my best to stay focused and do what I need to do. Over time I learned to talk myself out of reaching for an addiction until the cravings grew to be less. Luckily, my hard addictions were in my early twenties. I got it all out of my system so to speak, yet the addictive behavior is still there just below the surface. I have mastered the art of keeping it tempered and quiet through daily work, discipline, and effort over the years.

Many well-known artists, musicians, and actors are unable to control the input of stimuli and information, which tampers with their psyche. This drives them to drug, alcohol, or any other addiction to numb it all. One of the ways to avoid falling into an ocean of addiction is to find avenues to channel your creativity and gifts in a positive way. Take up a side hobby to unleash your positive gifts through an artistic endeavor. I worked with a well-known actress for many years who paints when she's not acting in front of the camera. Painting is another form of creative expression and it keeps her busy during those lulls between films, since you're not working every single day as an actor.

Actors feel more in control when they are working and inhabiting a character on stage or film. This keeps them out of trouble to an extent. If they're not working, which many are not on a regular basis, many of them find other positive avenues of creative expression. When you are working on a creative project, you are less likely to resort to addictive substances during those lulls. Creative expression brings you joy and an internal rushed high feeling that raises your vibration. This rush that you experience is your natural connection line with Heaven.

You may feel like an oddball or weird, but avoid placing too much emphasis on labeling yourself. Others may ridicule or criticize you for being different. They might call you inappropriate names, but pay no mind. It is better to be different than to be a clone that follows the herd. If you have a high receptivity to your environment, then you will want ensure that your surroundings are controlled and that you incorporate some measure of discipline. If you have too much rigid control, then this can inhibit your artistic creative side. Finding a happy balance with everything in life is what contributes to a positive energy flow. Be expressively creative while running your life like a strict executive.

The negatives that happen to this are that creative types are also all about experiencing and experimenting to one degree or another. It's best to work on keeping your research on a level that does not bring on an addiction. I am a writer, author, storyteller and entertainer. Couple that with research being my middle name and being a former addict with an ongoing addictive personality and you have a bit of rock and roll going on. I wouldn't just do something new a little bit. I would do it to the point of becoming an obsessive-compulsive mess. The one positive about that is I'd grow bored with it and kick it out of my system. If my soul is going to have an Earthly life, then it wants to know what is available in the physical world. This is to also have a greater understanding of the nature of it. One can study something, but it isn't the same as diving into it like a method actor.

Artistic pursuits and creative expression is a great way to reduce or eliminate abundance blocks in your life. It's a positive healthy way to channel and direct negative, stifled, and stuck energy. By diving into creative pursuits, you're releasing the negative energy and these blocks in the process. You're also awakening your inner child, which resides in a higher state than your ego. Consider finding a creative hobby or interest that brings you joy. Creativity enhances your life force and lifts your confidence level. You may even find that your creative project soon turns into life purpose work where it brings in supplemental income or it becomes a full time self-employed career. Some creative pursuits can include hobbies such as photography, painting, writing, playing music, singing, dancing, puzzles, or any measure of arts and crafts.

Writing is a great way to be creative and express your inner self. You don't have to necessarily write a book. It can be something that you write for the sake of release. Writing is fantastic therapy! You can write your own manuscript or keep a regular journal. Join writing groups you feel comfortable in enough to share your work with others or to have a meeting with likeminded individuals that share your interests. If you're shy when it comes to in-person meetings or you don't have the time to travel to group settings, then look for online forums and groups where you can communicate on the Internet. This is one of the plusses to having access to technology.

You can keep a personal diary when you're going through transitions or just want to jot down day-to-day stuff. You can email it to yourself. For example, use the subject line: Diary+Date *(Diary 12-25-18)*. Jot down anything that comes to you about that day, what you're going through, and how you're feeling or anything at all, then email it to yourself. Create a folder in your email box marked "Journal" or "Diary" and file each one in there. Choose to do what you want with it at a later date or just keep it for your eyes only.

Every soul has some measure or range of creative gifts within them, even if you never honed in on that aspect of yourself. It might come out in ways that you never expected or in a manner that you wouldn't think to equate as one being creative. It comes out in a variety of ways such as being birthed out of the mundane and the practical. It can be the way you organize your house, to working on a puzzle, to taking that extra step to ensure that your emails are centered, justified, or in the right font. Creativity can be in the way you speak to others, whether that is on the phone, at your job, or on a stage to an audience.

Although the news media is responsible for a major influence on the darkness of one's ego in humanity, the media in general is a great outlet for a creative sensitive to pursue work in. Many have agreed to an Earthly life at this time in order to transmit their work in a much easier way than it would have been pre-Internet days. During pre-Internet days other people had a hold on preventing any creative artist from getting their work out to the public. Now most anyone can get their work out there with strong effort, diligence, and hard work. Depending on what your creative work entails, you may still need a team around you to some extent such as an agent, publicist, manager, etc.

While in one sense you are the manager of your life and your work, but in another it is helpful to have supportive professional objective parties around you for feedback when unleashing your art to the world. A friend is great to bounce stuff off of as long as the friend is someone you can trust. They are someone you can take constructive criticism from without getting upset or allowing it to damage your connection. The flip side is this friend should not be the type who is negative or jealous of you either. You likely being a sensitive should be able to pick up on any hint of dishonesty or malice from anyone when it comes to your art. It should be a given that you surround yourself with supportive friends, but sometimes even with the best supportive friendships they may develop resentment when they witness your success.

The one drawback to being able to put your creative work out into the world is marketing dollars. You can put your art into the world for sale, but if no one knows that it's out there and available, then it might feel as if your work was done for nothing. Unless you've got a huge trust fund or have made enough money at your day job to be able to do your creative life purpose work, then it can be challenging. True creative artists enjoy doing their work regardless of that. It's certainly helpful to have marketing dollars to promote your work or to make enough money with it where you can quit your day job. The creative artist that lives and breathes their work will still do it because they enjoy it. It's fulfilling and rewarding to them even if in the back of their mind they would like to make enough money to be able to do it full time.

Even if you are not immediately financially rewarded, take the time to acknowledge and recognize the beautiful work you've accomplished, as that will be its own reward. Give to yourself in some positive way for every job well done. Celebrate the accomplishments you do including the small ones. This assists in boosting your self-worth and vibration, which are both magnets for attracting in good stuff!

Be your most genuine and real self, but this goes without saying that your work should also be authentic. Authenticity is you being your most honest self without fear of judgment or criticisms. Avoid making changes or compromising because someone disagrees with any part of who you are and how you choose to express that. At the same time understand the benefits of constructive feedback, but don't marinate in it to the point where you feel it's negotiating how you express your artistic truth. When you bargain this honesty, then the heart essence put into the work is lost. It doesn't feel right and nor does it feel like you. You want to step away from the drama surrounding that. This is in order to clear your mind when you find that you're moving into people pleasing to make others happy.

Find the right balance between accepting others feedback and keeping your work genuine. The point of getting a second pair of objective eyes on your work put out to the public is because when you're heavily mired in a project or anything for that matter, then you don't necessarily see the possible hidden mistakes that could be present. There is a benefit to having compassionate, yet helpful input. Ask your Spirit team to guide you to the right people who can give honest feedback. There is a surplus of websites and companies devoted to offering services of every variety for a small fee. Sometimes this is the best route over giving it to a friend or acquaintance, since that becomes a conflict of interest. The one hired is objective and emotionally detached from what you're doing. This makes it a great test to see how a stranger reacts to it since your work is going out to strangers in the end as it is.

There will be times where it can be challenging to get motivated to do something you love. There are a variety of factors that could contribute to a lack of motivation. You're overworked, tired, stressed, depressed or have no support system. You have too much going on in your life around you. This is tampering chaotic and distractive energy enclosing in on your mind that it's difficult to find that space where motivation resides.

Some ways to get motivated are through relaxation. Take a time out to clear your space and remove any excess noise and distraction energy around you whether that is from people, your schedule, to any technological devices such as your phone or Internet. Turn off or temporarily remove phone apps that you hang out on to the point that you find that it occupies a great deal of your time. These are time wasters that block creative flow.

Sometimes doing busy work can help motivate you to do what you really want to do, because it's getting your mind charged up. Creative people understand this concept, since they have wrestled with creative blocks at one time or another. A writer is ready to sit down and start writing, but experiences a block having no clue what to write about. What do they do? They might clean the house, dust, vacuum, and organize. There are positive benefits to this, which includes implementing Feng Shui.

Feng Shui is an ancient Chinese art that contributes to the positive flow of good energy moving through all aspects of your life including your home and your soul. Some hire a professional Feng Shui artist to help them organize their home. This includes setting up your furniture in a manner that assists in attracting in good fortune. In the case where you're doing the busy work that consists of cleaning your house, this helps with the positive flow of energy, but isn't necessarily the art of Feng Shui. It's still an encouraging step in the right direction.

Writing or creating in a clean organized environment contributes to more precise focus, relaxation, motivation, and it helps in attracting in success. You want to make sure you don't find that you've wasted hours on this busy work. You've grown so good at cleaning the house that the day is over and you have no energy left to create. To get motivated takes discipline and you have to manage your life and the decisions you make like a top business executive.

Feeling overwhelmed can prevent you from finding that spark of motivation. You're looking far out in the distance at the end result of what you want to do. This makes the goal seem daunting or intimidating, so you talk yourself out of doing it and putting it off. Breaking your ultimate goal into baby steps is a great way to go.

I will at times call on the Archangel Uriel who lights the path that is unseen. Archangel Uriel will show me one step at a time when working on a book. I'll be asked to cover one topic, and then once that's accomplished he illuminates the next step. Before I know it what I set out to achieve is complete.

Uriel offers awesome creative impressions by dropping these light bulb ideas into your mind. You might have a creative idea, but then you grow overwhelmed as to how you're going to accomplish it. This is because you're seeing it far out in the distance, which can feel overwhelming. Take it one small step at a time and try not to think of the end result. This is a delay tactic the ego will impose upon you by making you believe that it's not possible to do. A rock climber understands its goal is to reach the top, but they're focusing on one step climb upwards at a time. They're not thinking, "I've got to get up there to the top. That seems so far. I can't do it."

Others complain about what's going on in their life and how it is not up to their standards. I ask them if they've asked for help. They will say, "Oh you're right! Okay, I will do that."

Talk to your Spirit team regularly and ask for help as needed, including with creative ideas. When you notice there is no movement and you begin to feel discouraged, then ask Heaven to boost your faith and show you signs that movement is forthcoming.

Signs and symbols are put in your path by your Spirit team to let you know they are with you and do hear your requests. It can also be to give you clues as to what they are trying to communicate to you. When you're ferociously requesting help and wondering if you're being heard, they will do things such as drop feathers, objects of meaning, or coins around you to let you know they got your message. Since they cannot pick up the phone to call you or send you an email, they resort to manipulating the energy in order to let you know they hear you loud and clear, or to get a specific message across. You are not being ignored and that should bring you peace of mind.

The Personal Altar

Creating a personal altar or space is a wonderful way to rouse your creativity. Awakening the creative part of you is beneficial because it unleashes pent up closed off repression. When left unchecked this can be a breeding ground for illnesses, diseases, and other negative attributes. There are hundreds of ways to begin the process of setting the creative part of you free. Creating a personal altar is one way, as it can be used as a place of focus when you're in a scattered state. This altar can be used for whatever you choose. Many spiritual people like to create this space for prayer, meditations, or readings. You decide what you will use it for.

Find a space or a corner in your home somewhere to set up a small table, which you will use to place important sacred items on that have meaning to you. You can place candles on it, crystals, divination tools, incense, sage, flowers, and/or little statues of deities that have some significance to you. When you create your sacred space, you will want to cleanse and purify it on occasion. You can do this by sage smudging. Light a bit of sage and move it all around you, then the table and area. Say a mental prayer with the intention that you are clearing this space of any lower energies allowing only the light to enter. You can use this space for prayer, to connect, to meditate, to get focused, or for whatever you choose.

Because this is a sacred space, you will want to ensure that it is protected. This means not only clearing it through prayer or the occasional sage smudging, but avoid placing other items on it. You're rushing around or you come home from work and immediately toss your car keys onto the sacred space table. Treating the space as a sacred one means you keep it protected and clear of other energies. When you toss your car keys on it, you're contaminating the sacred space with any negative energy that latched itself onto the keys. When you're driving the busy roads, then you're picking up on other energies such as abusive drivers or toxic people in other cars passing you. Ensure that you avoid putting anything else on the table that is not considered sacred to you.

The Joy of Receiving

Give yourself a break and practice the joy and love of receiving. Many spiritual or compassionate people have the qualities of being a selfless giver. While this is a magnificent heavenly trait to have, you can create an imbalance when that is all you are doing. In order to bring balance into your life, be open to receive in your life as well. When someone wants to do something nice for you for a change, then welcome that with open arms. Those that are predominately givers tend to wrestle with the joy of receiving. They might fall into the category of someone taking advantage of them.

Receiving is also giving to yourself where you are the receiver. It's treating yourself to something you love such as a weekend getaway somewhere or a spa day if you enjoy being pampered. Whatever it is that makes you smile to receive, then go for it and give to yourself.

When you balance giving and receiving gestures, then this uplifts your mood, raises your vibration, and awakens your inner child that is bursting with creativity. If you are the kind of person who gives too much or receives without giving, then this creates an imbalance in your life. Work on balancing the giving part of your nature with receiving.

Sometimes you work hard feeling like you're being ignored, or that there are no blessings coming in from this hard work. A possible block is the negative feeling you're experiencing. Deep inside you feel undeserving of blessings on some level. Know that you deserve blessings of abundance and good. Allow Heaven to bestow you with compensation for what you contribute to others and the world. When you open your arms to receive abundance, then it is easier to assist others after you're taken care of first.

You also don't want to spread yourself too thin where you constantly drop everything to help a friend, loved one, or family member whenever they ask. If you're not taken care of or in a comfortable place, then you feel resentful for having to help. Receiving is just as important as giving. Therefore, ensure there is a healthy balance on both ends. Put down strict boundaries to ensure that no one takes advantage of your good nature.

CHAPTER TEN

Rise Into Creative Confidence

Introverted and shy people have a higher quotient of creativity flowing through their spirit. Someone can be an introvert, but not shy, whereas an extrovert can be shy. Someone shy might be misconstrued to be an introvert when that's not always the case. Introverts keep to themselves or prefer higher bouts of alone time than an extrovert. It can be difficult for them to connect with others even if they crave human stimulation once in awhile. They may also have trouble allowing their fearless assertive confidence to shine out, but the exception is when they are engaging creatively. There are many ways that an introverted creative soul can connect with other likeminded people. Technology has its cons, but there are the obvious benefits to devices such as social media or phone apps. You can take your time getting to know others on a phone app or a social media page before you are comfortable enough to take it to the next level. The next steps preceding that are personal email, text, and then phone conversations. If you cannot have a phone conversation, then how are you going to be making it through an in person hang out? The next step is followed by meeting in person. All of this can help ease someone into confidence.

Other ways of connecting with those like you is to take a class. This can be online or a physical classroom, which allows you to interact with other students. Taking a class in the area or genre of your interest assists in awakening the confident creative part of you. It also opens the door to getting to know others with similar interests.

When you communicate via social media or a phone app, then be sure to put in an effort with others by opening up beyond a few words. I've discovered through hands on research that people who reach out to me barely put in more than a one to five word sound bite response that is similar to the person before them. If you're a highly creative soul, then this shouldn't be too much of an issue since you can find creative ways to string words together to catch the other person's attention. The most nerve wracking challenge will be when you and this other person meet face to face, but by that time you'll likely be so familiar with each other that it won't be that difficult. This is pending you're not jumping to meet every single person the second they message you.

Some of the other positive benefits to following social media pages or taking classes in the area of your interest are that higher learning and interacting with other like minded souls stimulates inspiration. It pulls you out of a lull you might be experiencing and activates your mind while raising your energy levels, and focus.

Inspiration is a key component to achieve when looking to get creative. Find ways to bring on inspiration such as taking regular time outs to walk through a nature setting. Take long weekend getaways to a serene place of your choice that can inspire you. Any place bathed in nature can help with inspiration from the beach, mountains, desert, lakes, or any open nature preserve with little to no people. Go to a museum, art gallery, listen to motivating music, read a book, or watch a movie. Those are some of the things I do to get inspired. I also find inspiration in other people. My love relationships, romantic dates, and friendships have helped me creatively by acting as a muse.

Expressing Your Soul Through Creativity

The soul starves for stimulation and creativity. Express yourself artistically without censure or fear that others will not approve or like what you do. You don't have to share your art with the world if you choose not to. It can be for your eyes only, something you share with a loved one, or your close trusted circle around you. This is assuming that those who are immediately close to you are people you can trust and express yourself freely with. I've discovered from being approached by readers that they've said they feel they can be more open with me who is a stranger than someone in their immediate circle. One should have at least one person in their life they can completely trust until the end of their days. Work on getting to know other people through social media pages, classes, destinations, and apps that promote positive common interests between you.

Unleashing the creative spirit in you contributes to confident soul success in your life. Creative people seek out ways to stimulate that part of their soul for the sake of release. When done positively you engage in activities that are stimulating to your mind. A successful soul reads, researches, and partakes in positive activities, while an unsuccessful soul is sedentary, surfs the Internet, or sits around drinking bottles of alcohol, watching television all day, or chatting with others on apps out of boredom. When the darkness attaches itself to you, then this expands the ego causing one to go on a rant, rave, and attacking frenzy on social media through comments and posts. Now you've officially moved into the darkness of ego.

The Darkness of Ego

I've been doing extensive research into the human condition since childhood. This is due to my fascination with the complexities of human beings the same way a scientist examines a specimen in a bottle.

Heaven watched the rise of technology bring down the masses. No one reads as much anymore, educates themselves, or takes the time to walk in someone else's shoes. If you believe in something they don't, then they take it upon themselves to send you a toxic negative diatribe against you. They follow and adopt whatever the media or their peers feed them and believe it to be Gospel. Many will read a headline and base their opinion on what the headline is telling them without researching the story beyond the piece. If you're that rattled about a headline, then it must be something that hits home to you. If that's the case, then why not research more heavily into that topic and make it your life's purpose work to help instead of attack.

There are few that can carry deep compassionate meaningful conversations even if you disagree with someone. Arguing and antagonism is at the forefront instead of calm, balanced, compassionate conversations about differences in views and opinions.

There is no exploration, intelligence, or branching away from the crowd to investigate, research, and discover the deeper answers because no one cares. Attention spans are stunted and posting sound bites is in to get likes and followers.

Conversations fizzle out as quickly as they start up, which has all carried over to the demise of long term love relationships causing many of them to be short lived.

People today have a harder time working together in a union for life. There is too much ego to include another person's feelings and desires. You get into relationships to help the soul learn valuable traits such as compromise, balance, love, forgiveness, and on and on. It should not be about what can you do for me, but what can I do for you and for us?

Arguments are made to justify egotistical selfish behaviors. It is designed to mask the fact that the reasons long term relationships don't last is because people have short attention spans and grow bored with what they have after five minutes. No one cares about anybody or anything anymore. They pretend to when someone famous dies for a couple of days, but then they're obsessing over the next big media story. They're governed by their ego and what they desire at that moment. If it's no longer on par with the one they're with, then they leave them instead of compromising and finding a middle ground. They end up with someone new that lasts for a short time and that ends the same way. It's a repetitive cycle that ceases to end. Those that are single want to be in a relationship and those in a relationship fantasize about being single. The ego wants the opposite of what it has. All of this strangles the confident and poised creative spirit right out of you.

Ignore the Critics

Healthy creative souls are the ones more likely to compliment others on their positive traits, while unhealthy souls will criticize you, then post negative words online. The unhealthy unsuccessful soul sits around gossiping about people, while the successful soul is animated and excitedly discusses things they want to do and accomplish.

Diving into a creative project or functioning from the artistic side of you helps in removing blocks. These blocks prevent good stuff from flowing to you. It cuts off the communication connection line with your own spirit, and your team in Heaven.

If you're a creative soul that enjoys the creative process, but also sells your art to consumers, then you understand the dynamic beyond being creative in the privacy of your own home. Having a career in the creative arts makes you susceptible to criticism from the public. The irony is the creative person is also a deeply sensitive soul, so it's important to do your best in separating the reality of what you do from harsh critics. All that matters is you participate in work that is meaningful to you. The ones it will benefit will be guided to it. There will be always be negative naysayers that have something toxic to say about your efforts, but their opinion has no validity in the eyes of God. When you put your soul's expression out into the world, then release the desire to absorb any criticism that happens to come your way. As for any measure of success you crave from your work, side business, or hobby, keep the faith that it will happen.

Remain optimistic while you continue working at your hobby and art. If it's something you enjoy doing, then it won't feel like work to you. You'll do it regardless if there is any monetary gain in it. Many success stories from popular artists admit that the success came to them out of nowhere. Suddenly they began to see a gradual rise or immediate shot of financial success fly into their life. When you love and enjoy what you're doing, then you're infusing this love enjoyment energy into your work. This is a positive ingredient that will attract a like minded energy to it. If you do your work with fear and worry, then you will attract that kind of negative crowd base to it. The energy will be a block that prevents success from entering the picture. Stay positive, optimistic, and joyful with all that you do when you can help it. At the same time the more successful you become, then the more good and bad you will receive. You grow to be exceptionally great at ignoring the critics.

I receive my fair share of criticism, although it is minimal in comparison to those that appreciate who I am or my work. I've been receiving harsh criticism from others since I was a kid. By the time I became an author, I was already indifferent and detached from those that take issue with what I do, how I do it, or who I am. I've never cared if someone doesn't like me or not. I'm not going to stop because of them. I own my life and I live it for me. If I don't care about something or someone, I don't give it any energy or attention. It's not interesting enough for me to bother.

I've worked with well known talent during my tenure in the Entertainment business. These actors have told me they know to stay away from reading gossip about themselves or read comments under articles about them. I've never heard of any cases where they fold and read any of that stuff. Most of them are too productive and busy to notice. When you're busy with life you don't have time for boredom that leads to reading negative stuff about oneself. Not only are the comments and articles not based in reality, but it's not healthy or beneficial for you on any level to soak in that energy.

I've witnessed what it's like from the perspective of a famous artist. To me they're no different than any other friend or colleague, but then you realize they are super popular and many in the world love and admire their work. There are just as many people in the world who despise or criticize them unfairly and negatively. They say things about them that are not true, but you ignore that and stay focused on what's important. It's like someone saying negative toxic things on the news about someone you're close to. You don't know why or where that's coming from. It appears bizarre and peculiar that a stranger is talking about someone they know nothing about personally. It's also always been inaccurate.

Avoid allowing anyone to stop you from doing what you love. Ignore the naysayers and stay strong in faith knowing that you are loved no matter what you do or who you are. There will always be a critic out there who has something to say.

Focus on your work, put confidence into what you're creating in life, then put it out into the world if that's what you choose to do. When you release it into the world, you're also releasing the need to concern yourself over anyone who happens to like it or not. You create your art for yourself, and then you share it with those in the world who are interested and positively benefit from it. There will always be someone who doesn't like you, or what you do, so you have to get over that. It's not your issue to wrestle with.

Steer clear of all drama and negativity in others around you. This includes strangers who criticize you – not to mention those who are allegedly intended to be close to you. There is a difference between helpful constructive criticisms from those around you as opposed to critical attacks from strangers. The difference is that constructive criticism is someone who is close to you who've you asked their opinion on something and they've given you a critique.

Constructive criticism comes from a place of love where the person wants you to succeed. The opposite side of this kind of criticism is someone who is jealous of who you are and what you can do. They attack instead of offering helpful comments that benefit, because they have venom over who you are and what you're accomplishing. The lower self is governed by the Darkness and wants to take you down, but the higher self is of God and the Light and wants to see you succeed.

There are some people that are afraid to dive into anything artistic related for fear of criticism.

The more you do something, then the easier it gets and the better you are at it. This can be anything in life from a job you take that you've never done before. You dread being exposed and vulnerable as if you're in some form of danger due to your high sensitivity. This anxiety is part of your ego mind and not based in truth. Avoid altering your creative work to appeal to the masses or out of panic that someone won't like it. When you do that you are distancing yourself from authenticity. This is seen with popular music acts that conform to the current market to remain significant to popular culture at that time instead of creating authentically the way they did when they first started their career. They were a trendsetter and unique when they weren't attempting to people please.

Your creative spirit is intended to be solely you and who you are buried deep within, and not what someone else wants or will want to see. If they want to see something, then let them create their own thing. This isn't about creating art that you intend to sell, but this is anything you set out to do whether it's a job, a friendship, or relationship. Be your most authentic self since you can only fake it for so long before being found out. Your authentic self is far greater than any fickleness.

I've done work that I've kept on a shelf for longer than it should have due to my insane unrealistic need for perfectionism. It's a level that no one can get to. If I waited until that thoroughness was there, then I would never get any work done. My Spirit team taught me in the beginning of my days to release the need to be perfect. The only thing that matters is the content and what one chooses to say. While it should be somewhat digestible, avoid getting lost over the fact that something might be in the wrong place. Make it as good as you can and then move onto something else. If you get into your head wondering what if no one likes it, then just quit, lie down, and wait to die. It's a waste of time putting something off because you're not ready or it will never be perfect. What is considered perfect is based on human ego rules, which have no validity in the end anyway. You have your own individual stamp on what you choose to say or create. It is impossible to please every single person. It will never happen no matter what you do, so throw that idea out the window and just do what feels right to you in the end.

Be Your Confident Authentic Self

Your sensitivity is a gift that can be immersed into your creative work. Other sensitive's will pick up on if you're going against who you are to please the crowd as opposed to be your true self. They will be attracted to you and your work when you do not compromise your integrity. Not only will they be fascinated, but they will relate and enjoy you even more for this authenticity.

I was seventeen when I obtained my first job. It was the one I honed in on and wanted with incredible force. Not many can say that as a teenager. You usually just accept any job you can get. I thought, "I need a job and the one I want right now is that one." After much persuasion on my part with the supervisor, she folded and hired me. I wasn't worried if I could do the job, but instead I was excited to learn how to do it. Soon I was mastering it as I mastered all jobs over the course of my life. When I got into the film business when I was twenty-three I feared I would be fired in the first week. The opposite ended up happening where I became a sought after commodity behind the scenes for studios, production companies, and talent. This is because I was soon doing the job with extreme precision and confidence. Word was spreading fast in this circus of similar creative intelligent misfits. Incidentally some of the well-known movie stars I know and have worked with also shared with me that they also had worry in the beginning of a film shoot. Some privately admitted they thought they would get fired. This gave me piece of mind that if someone that worldly known at their craft still has those worries, then this is a human nature trait that can attack anyone of any stature.

The same fighting confident nature is applied to all areas of extracurricular work I've done. I wanted to try my hands at those jobs for the experience and knowledge it entailed ranging from real estate, to law, and to digital marketing. All of my past jobs were classes that I received financial compensation for. When I started each gig I didn't know anything about the genre. I was hired based on my enthusiasm and creative nature. When I chose to dissolve the employment in those arenas I did it at a point where I was on top of my game and had fully mastered the genre. All of those classes infused creative knowledge that I could impart into my work as a self employed author. Everything you experience helps you gain confidence, knowledge, and life lessons. These traits were applied to my past love relationships where I would give my full confident work into the connection.

You deserve all measures of success whether that is inner or outer achievement. You are a soul child born with an innate knowing how to create. When you're home in Heaven on the Other Side, you paint the pictures of what you desire with intention. It is almost like magic due to how effortless it is. For instance in the spirit world, if you want to visit someone or go somewhere, you think it and you are instantly there. The soul is limitless in the spirit world, while the soul is imperfect in the physical human body. On Earth, you can't think I want to be in Bali right now and then get transported there. The manifestation process on Earth is you can think about being in Bali today, then eventually one day get there with fearless assertive confidence that you will. Your thoughts produce circumstances as long as its consistent. When you think or dream positive things, then that energy is catapulted outwardly and returned back to you tenfold. This is why you want to make sure you stay as positive as you can. Release any negative self-defeating words from your mind and aura. Know that you deserve good just as much as anyone that has experienced popular success.

Unleash Your Soul's Creative Essence

Allow the vibrating power of spirit to flow through you and awaken the creative part of your soul. Take care of yourself on all levels inside and out. This will assist in giving you greater energy, stamina, and focus, not to mention a stronger connection with your Spirit team. Having a crystal clear communication line with God will enable you to make sounder decisions in your life. It will assist you in reaching a higher vibration state than if you didn't have that connection. Creativity helps in raising your vibration into higher feelings of joy, love, and peace, while boosting your faith and optimism. Diving into creative projects or obtaining a creative slant in your nature and day to day dealings also help in lifting blocks that are in your way towards abundance enlightenment.

Pay attention to the guidance your Spirit team filters in through you. When you receive a sign or message that is continuous, then this is a clue that it could be Heavenly support coming into you. The message has a positive uplifting feeling to it and will not be bathed in fear or anxiety. Sometimes one can mistake a message for being heavenly support as opposed to their ego. Heavenly support has a high vibration positive feeling to it that benefits you and everyone around.

Expressing restlessness or any uncomfortable feeling through creativity is a fantastic way to release negativity from your soul. You can paint, draw, take photos, write, play music, games, make your own mix MP3's or CD's, re-organize your home, put puzzles together, make fun videos, sing, dance, or anything creative at all. All creative movements get the positive energy within and around you moving again.

Awakening the creative spirit in you is more than working on art projects or becoming an entrepreneur and opening up your own business. Those traits are part of it, but it is also unleashing that part of you that is connected to God. It is the creative part of you within that is in tune to all nuances in and around you. It is your inner child that is full of love, joy, and peace around the clock. This is why detoxing and watching what you ingest are beneficial. These all play a factor into what drains your life force energy zapping any ounce of creativity in you.

Take care of all parts of you. Watch what you ingest and the energy of the thoughts you put into your mind. Self care is a not only a luxury, but a necessity. Love all that you are and remember to pat yourself on the back for any job well done. When you've accomplished anything at all, then treat yourself to something good in celebration. Whether that's a hiking sabbatical trip or that t-shirt or music album you always wanted. Go for it! Reward yourself. You deserve the endless reservoirs of success and prosperity in all areas of your life that exist. Never stop being creative and live your life from the heart. Create out of love and give out of love.

CHAPTER ELEVEN

Balancing Healthy Selfishness and Selflessness

In the next two chapters will look at the differences between key traits that many vacillate between. When you understand the differences between something like healthy selfishness and selflessness, as well as aggression, passive aggression, and assertiveness, then the more you are able to stand in your own Divine confident power.

Coming to the end of the road as you close your Earthly life chapter up, you realize then if you hadn't before that it was always intended to be about love. Your soul was born from a source of love and you will die right back into that love. Love is the most powerful energy foundation that exists in all dimensions. It is what helps you manifest fearless assertive confidence from within. The only thing that matters in the end is love. The best way to channel energy positively is to remember all things connected to love. Love is what kills energy like anger, sadness, fear, and worry. Outstretch your arms, release any fears, and fall back into the arms of this love. Allow it to protect and guide you on your Earthly journey.

Bring your soul to that beautiful glorious space of centeredness, serenity, and peace. Ignore any drama swirling around you and view circumstances from an emotionally detached perspective without judgment. Increase your faith through prayer and regular conversations with the Divine, knowing and understanding that you are loved and watched over.

Every day should be the most magical time of the year, but the lack of love on the planet that continues to be prevalent makes it less enchanting. Love and accept others even if their values are differing from yours. This is easier said than done since many have forgotten about the basic concept of what love is. Humanity continues to have a long way to go before every soul on the planet is aware that it's about love. One might say that it's the other person that isn't displaying love, but two wrongs don't make a right. Someone has to get the ball rolling in displaying love.

Treat everyone with kindness and compassion even if they don't share your values. This goes for all sides of the spectrum since everyone becomes guilty of it at one time or another. It's not okay to treat others badly or to abuse the luxuries you've been given as a free will thinking conscious being.

It's one thing to defend yourself from someone who has accosted or randomly disrespected you, but it's another to take it upon yourself to harass someone because they're different and not a clone of you. You reach no middle ground when you're that rigid.

The #1 trait that Spirit doesn't like to see is someone mistreating or disrespecting another person in any form. This means a certain amount of decorum and etiquette is something they prize. Mistreatment is considered one of the most distasteful quality traits for God to witness. Sadly that's also the top trait displayed on the planet by humankind.

There are different shades of mistreatment and disrespect that exist. Someone treated you unkindly, then the natural immediate reaction is to be reactive or defensive, so you lash out in retaliation. There's also that fine line between how far you intend to go with mistreating another person to deciding to limit your reactions to slights on your ego by choosing your battles wisely and selectively.

Some refuse to give respect to those that are mean to them, which is not what Spirit is saying. Decorum and etiquette more or less point to the same thing. This is about exuding class, compassion, and grace, while giving off a certain level of respect towards others. Humanity has a long way to go with that. There are a great deal of tantrums and stomping around angrily when someone doesn't get their way instead of seeking out the middle ground in meeting others half way.

Treat people with kindness and compassion, but it's understandable to defend yourself with assertive confidence if someone attacks you.

One hopes that with age comes wisdom and spiritual maturity, but as you know this is not necessarily the case. In your twenties, you are more likely to be angrily reactive over something than a wiser one moving into their thirties and beyond. This is because the older you get, whether in human age or soul age, you hopefully learned to incorporate more of the Divinely guided traits of patience, forgiveness, and humility. What can you let go of, get over, and move on from? The risk you run into when not getting over something is when you fall into perpetual antagonism. Not only does that create enormous weight on your spirit, which can cause damage to your health and Divine connection line, but there comes a point when no one is being helped by the repetitive antagonism.

On the one hand Spirit says to teach people how to respect others, but you also can't get swept away in the noise nonsense. The noise nonsense is ranting and raving with everyone else on social media over the top trending story. That kind of disrespect doesn't do anything except add to the drama and noise. The mistreatment and disrespect here in Spirit's case is primarily the one on one kind, even though all forms of mistreatment are unacceptable to them. This can be where someone has overstepped their boundaries or is not displaying appropriate compassionate assertive protocol.

The worst kind of mistreatment is abuse of any

kind whether that's physical, emotional, psychological, and so on. This is what irks and pains Spirit to witness, because in the end whatever you're not able to get over doesn't matter in spiritual truth, since you and all of this will one day cease to exist. To God all that's seen is everyone disrespecting everybody else with no end in sight. That energy is darting all over the place. At that point, there is no valid reason for it so just stop.

The most spiritual evolved soul is guilty of it too. Every soul on the planet is at one time or another, but they're aware of what Spirit doesn't like to see and wants to see more of. This statement isn't cut and dry as it can go exceptionally in depth when looking at each case. The general consensus for Spirit has always been the same. Treat your neighbor with respect even if you personally disagree with them. That's a rough trait for all to observe, but one to remember to revert to whenever possible. This is not about taking abuse. This is for those that deliberately and intentionally cause turmoil in others. Disrespect and mistreatment should never be tolerated. If that means you need to rise into Divine warrior mode to stomp that out, then that is what you must do. You have to teach people how to respect you.

In a perfect world, you wouldn't have to teach someone how to respect others, but the reality is there are billions of children on the planet that haven't been taught the basic concept of respect. If it's not there, then you need to move on. This is also about someone that physically, psychologically, emotionally, or verbally assaults you, then they need to be taught the meaning of respect. This isn't through the means of violence. You have to stand up for yourself when possible.

A five-year-old boy was brutally tortured and abused by his parents to the point where he fell into a coma, then passed away. Those parents need to learn the art of respect and compassion for human life. Walking away from something like that is not an option. There are cases where certain behavior needs to be taught and corrected.

Avoiding someone that mistreats or disrespects you is always the first way to go. This is especially the case with online bullies that take it upon themselves to message a stranger through social media to attack them. You don't bother with that kind of nonsense, but block them instead and move on. Flick them off your shoulder as if it's a bee. When one is in situations where that's not feasible or logical, such as a continuously hostile boss, an abusive spouse, or someone you're living with that perpetually antagonizes you, then there is no choice, but to talk to them and train them how to respect you. Otherwise you will end up spending each day under the reigns of abuse, which ultimately causes all sorts of psychological damage that is difficult to repair.

If someone attacks you online, then you ignore that energy, you don't engage with it. You avoid, delete, block, and move on to more important things. If you did something that instigated mistreatment from someone around you, then be conscious of when you did that and take steps to mend or correct it. Sometimes one can unknowingly hurt someone's feelings without realizing that's what may have caused them to be disrespectful towards you. People are complicated beings and learning to discern when a situation warrants how you'll react in kind to a disrespectful person requires your keen intuitive radar where you also choose your battles wisely.

The ultimate reason all are here is to love and to learn how to love. You cannot learn that unless you're thrown onto a planet with others who are different from you. Learn to accept others and see someone's personal truth. You're not saying you agree with them, but a way shower illuminates the way by example.

Be the King or Queen of showing respect and compassion to others. These traits are not popular globally. This doesn't mean that if someone abuses or walks all over you that you take it lying down. Pick your battles wisely and use assertiveness over aggressiveness when slighted. The general demeanor to strive for on a regular basis as much as possible is respect and compassion. Being a compassionate loving person is what garners real attention and attraction from others. If that turns someone off, then don't allow them into your auric circle.

Divine Act of Selflessness

Being entirely selfless is an act that requires no personal gratification, but there is some measure of fulfillment with the act of selflessness. You require unconditional love in a relationship, but unconditional love is to love without conditions. Most everybody has conditions to one an extent or another. This is especially the case in intimate romantic relationships. You hope the person you're with doesn't cheat or isn't abusive. Those are highly reasonable and warranted conditions, but they are conditions. You can get close to unconditional love as much as you can get close to selflessness.

All human beings have both a light and dark ego. The light ego is connected to traits such as having confidence in your abilities, while the dark ego is bogged down in gossip, anger, judgment, or violence. The dark ego will aggressively attack someone, but a light ego will assertively communicate their point. Those who are typically giving by nature are not being altruistic for personal pleasure, but for spiritual nourishment. There are various levels of attainment when it comes to altruism. To be completely selfless is a Divine act possible to achieve. You are made in the likeness of His being. Therefore, you have the capacity of great love and immense selflessness built within you.

I've witnessed others reach that space of being completely selfless. They've personally done things to help others without the longing for any kind of gain. No gratitude is required in those instances. The selfless soul desires to make sure someone is taken care of without any fanfare or acknowledgment. Because why offer praise for displaying traits that are present in every soul on the planet.

At the same time, many long for some measure of approval from others. Even the most centered person on the planet doesn't mind the occasional validation, which acts more as confirmation that they're on the right track. This doesn't make them any less insecure, but it does serve as a reminder to them that the work they're doing isn't for nothing. They can more than likely live life without it after a certain point. When you're in your teens and twenties you generally long for more validation and approval than when you age beyond that.

Altruism or selflessness is part of the universal truth, but it's also a God given trait you were born with. It's universal truth only to the extent that humankind decided to make the act of being selfless a virtue. A universal truth is everyone agreeing to make something be of truth at that time in history. This has been altered as humankind progressed onward. Universal truth is subjective, but basic core values are innately built into a soul operating at full capacity with a high vibration at optimum levels. Parts of the consciousness are God given qualities, while other parts are astrological and part of that person's human life upbringing during the crucial developmental years. It's a cocktail of complicated composites within each soul's make up.

Basic God given traits are displayed while in a high vibrational state. High vibrational states are qualities such as love, serenity, peace, confidence, compassion, and selflessness. The angels are egoless and therefore selfless requiring nothing in return for being selfless. They have nothing to gain by that action. They can be selfless due to being completely egoless. Human beings have an ego, so although many human beings can be selfless, there are varying levels of what constitutes observing selflessness.

Bright Side of Selfishness

If you believe someone else is selfish, then you may be projecting a lack that exists within you. You feel everyone owes you something, which is what selfishness is. You're threatened by someone who says what they want, does what they want, when they want, and without any interference. The person who is confident and goes after what they want, and who toots their own horn isn't concerned over what someone else thinks about them, especially a stranger's opinion. It will not sway the confident person that governs its life under the jurisdiction of the Light. Tooting your own horn isn't a spiritual crime. It can grow annoying for some on the receiving end when it's constant, but it's certainly not criminal. Most anyone with a social media account is praising themselves on some level. This is part of self-love, which is the opposite of low self-esteem and having no love for oneself.

An authentic selfish person has confidence and persistence. They're also less likely to be taken advantage of or give up on their goals. Selfish people have no guilt over saying no, while a narcissus will become angry when someone tells them no. Human ego trained one another to view selfishness as something negative. What some people see as selfishness, Heaven sees as self-love. Anyone calling you selfish prefers that you put yourself second and put them first, which falls into narcissism. True dark selfishness would fall more into greed. This would be racing past someone in a restaurant to get that great table before someone else takes it.

The opposite of being selfish is selfless, but you cannot be adequately selfless when you've fallen into people pleasing or emotional neediness. While in that state you become resentful that you're doing things for others and receiving nothing in return, which is not authentically selfless.

A selfish person takes care of its soul by instilling strict boundaries that prevent negative toxic people and energies from intruding on its serenity. Only when the selfish person is taken care of can they take care of others. The selfish are confident in what they want and go after it without any resistance.

The angels are selfless because they have no ego and aren't struggling to survive on a physical climate that demands you to be selfish and take care of you first. When a high vibrational soul has all they need to survive, then their focus grows more outwardly looking to see who they can help. You cannot achieve great heights or survive on the planet by being entirely selfless. That's not realistic or practical in a world full of people who are untrustworthy and will take advantage of your good nature for being selfless. They'll do it in a myriad of ways from insulting you to displaying passive aggressive behavioral traits in hopes they can get you to do something for them. A true healthy selfish person can see right through both and will have no trouble saying no without guilt.

You're moving into greedy territory when you use someone for your own gain. Being selfish is not a negative trait, because then it becomes greed in that instant. When a narcissus doesn't get what they want, or things don't go their way, they'll insist it's everyone else that is selfish only caring about themselves. You are not a victim and nobody owes you anything. You owe it to yourself to take care of you. You cannot place that kind of impossible demanding attention and love to be given to you by someone else. That's what God is for. Having confidence, integrity, strength, and going after what you want is healthy selfishness and self-love.

When you're selfish how would you know you acted selfishly? You are too self-absorbed and narcissistic to care. Learning to be selfless takes quite a bit of time. The selfish individual needs to want to become more selfless, but it's difficult for their ego to convince them that this is what should happen. There is a delicate balance between portraying both a healthy selfishness and selflessness.

How enticing it can be to attempt to keep people happy. Certain instances can call for you to people please, but if it means you're going against your higher self's integrity, or God and your Spirit team's warnings in order to do that, then your heading down precarious ground. This will create unnecessary chaos that is avoidable when you follow the wisdom you receive from above.

CHAPTER TWELVE

Assertiveness, Aggression, Passive Aggression

When one is angry or upset, the human ego will display three different traits: Aggression, passive-aggression, or assertiveness.

The highest and most effective energy form of getting your point across when you're upset or need to correct a wrong is by displaying assertiveness.

Aggression is being directly hostile when you confront someone. You're a militant bully with the mantra that it is your way or the high way and no other opinion is allowed. Aggression primarily comes from fear or ego. It is fear that you are not being heard or the person you're directing that aggression towards is not going to listen to you. It can also come from high anxiety brought on in artificial ways such as consuming too much caffeine where you're bouncing all over the place in agitated aggression.

Aggressive force is your ego wanting to make sure that the person you're directing this force towards understands that you are in charge. You will convey that point by any means necessary. It's attempting to dominate someone with severe force to get that person to go along with your point.

Someone that screams their argument at someone else while pointing their finger repeatedly at you is someone displaying aggression. When you're aggressive you have a sense of entitlement with some self-righteousness mixed in.

A man sees someone moving in on his love partner, and the man becomes a bully and starts to physically shove the person who is making the move on his mate. This is aggressive behavior that can also be someone with high testosterone. Testosterone is built into the chemistry of the male species. Some have more of it than others and this can show through in their aggressive behavior. It can take a great deal of focus and discipline to try and keep that under control as much as possible. I definitely understand since it's been known that I can be pretty aggressive at times. It is instinctual in the male species to react aggressively to ensure others understand you've marked your territory. It also tends to be stronger in men in their teens and especially twenties. As they age their testosterone begins to decline and so does their aggressive behavior.

Passive aggression is just as bad as aggression, except that passive aggression is indirect. You're upset with a love partner, but you don't say anything or tell them that you are angry or bothered by something they did. Instead you keep it bottled up until it explodes in underhanded ways. The passive aggressive person will pout and mope whenever you're around. You'll sense something is wrong, but when you ask them if everything is okay, they appear cold and distant holding in their emotion. They may bite back under their breath with, "I'm fine."

They throw up a wall that makes them inaccessible and thus becoming submissive. This person may have lower testosterone and more estrogen, but they could also be more sensitive or afraid of confrontation erupting. Your thoughts and feelings do matter. It's important to express them when possible by being assertive.

The male species typically has a good deal of testosterone and therefore comes off aggressive when upset, while the female species has more estrogen and therefore can come off passive aggressive when upset. Either gender has displayed both aggression and passive aggression regardless of how much testosterone or estrogen one has. The reasoning for laying out the examples in this way is a generality. This way of reacting to something one is upset about is part of the human make-up, but it is one that can be reined in. Men see a drop in their testosterone levels as they age, while women see a drop in their estrogen levels and rise in testosterone.

I was jogging through a quiet residential area at night and suddenly a dog came at me. I stopped abruptly thrown off guard and hopped back a couple steps. A woman yanked her dog back with the leash at the same time. The woman said with warmth and kindness, "Don't you mind him, he just likes you cause you've got a lot of testosterone."

When active men continuously work out and exercise it starts to raise their testosterone levels. This can also contribute to the aggressiveness that comes out at times.

The passive aggressive person doesn't necessarily communicate with you with words. When they do finally talk with you, they make comments that start to sound as if they are indirectly attacking you or giving you back handed compliments. It takes you awhile, maybe even weeks before you realize, "Wait a minute, you're mad at me. What's wrong?"

The partner exuding passive aggressive behavior is unable to articulate what's wrong, so they become aloof, cold, and distant with you. They might be sad and slouch whenever you're around. If you're a sensitive or someone in tune, then you can pick up on this energy like nobody's business. Someone not in tune has no clue the other person's mad, so it can take much longer to realize it.

Passive aggression also comes from fear where the person is afraid to voice what's wrong, as they don't want to rock the boat or start a fight. They're not fans of confrontation and it's easier to just not say anything and mope around the issue. The problem is that keeping this anger or upset inside for prolonged periods of time can fester and cause potential health issues. It's better to get it out even if someone doesn't want to hear it. You can articulate what's wrong with compassion and assertiveness.

If you're afraid to say something, then write it out. You don't have to email it to the person you're upset with. Email it to a trusted friend or to yourself. It's important to get those feelings out of you. Whenever one of my close friends we're going through a heartbreaking relationship split with someone who left them, they would have the urge to call the ex or send them an email full of angry and upset tirades. They would send it to me saying, "Should I send this to them?"

I'd of course say, "Oh no don't say that. Write out everything to your heart's content, but just send it to yourself or me, so you feel like you're getting it out of you."

Sometimes they would send it to me and then send it to their partner that left them as well. It always backfires in their face where they come back to me. "I should've listened to you. Now it's worse than ever!"

When someone has chosen to leave you, there is nothing you can do or say to change that person's mind. They've already decided and it's in motion. They've more than likely decided long before they took that step to let you in on it. It's best to give them what they want and that is to be separated from you. If it's meant to be, they will come back and then you can decide whether to go for another round or move on.

One thing to consider is that you should feel safe enough to talk openly with your love mate. A relationship is supposed to be you and this person against the world. If you can't talk about things openly with one another, then who can you talk to about that stuff?

Getting an aggressive person to calm down is challenging since the aggressive person is heated. When you are dealing with an aggressive person, you're dealing with someone disconnected from their centered higher self at that moment. They are in no position to reason with, so it's best to get out of their line of fire and wait until they cool off.

The passive aggressive person is challenging to deal with also, because the wall they put up is impossible to pull down in order to get them to open up. The person they're being that way with starts to feel rejected by them. This creates an even bigger distance between both people.

As I've grown older, I've found that I've been more successful at being assertive over aggressive, even though it will freely come out here and there. I've certainly also had moments of passive aggression, but that's mostly in past love relationships. I am a sensitive and did not want to rock the boat with the person I'm involved with. This stems from an abusive childhood where I was trained to go along with someone just to please the abusive person. It's taken a lifetime of working on dissolving that behavior.

In the end, most everyone displays aggression,

passive aggression, and assertiveness at one time or another. Be aware when you are displaying aggressive or passive-aggressive behavior, and then begin the process of shifting that energy into assertiveness.

An aggressive person may get violent or into derogatory name calling to get someone to hear their point. They might say to someone or write to someone on social media something like, "You're an (expletive)! Anyone with half a brain knows that doesn't work!"

Whereas someone that displays assertive behavior will speak the truth directly with strength, but it is intertwined with compassion and understanding where one is open to compromise. You're not talking at someone to force your beliefs down someone's throat. Instead the assertive person is talking with the other person as if they're on the same level.

An assertive person will say something like, "I understand your point, but it would be more effective if we did it this way, because then you're not excluding anybody."

A passive aggressive person wouldn't say anything even though they're bothered by something. They would willingly go along with what they disagree with even though deep down they're unhappy about it. No one would know they're unhappy about it, because the passive aggressive person isn't telling them they have a problem.

Assertiveness is the goal to thrive for when angry or upset about something. When you display assertiveness, then you accomplish what you want. An assertive person is firm, stands their ground, but they work with and include the other person they're attempting to come to a resolution with. The assertive person is calm, strong, and composed, but not unresponsive, which would be passive aggressive. They are also not a tough bully, which is aggression. The assertive person is a relaxed centered person who is also direct in their communication with what they want to accomplish. They speak clearly and concisely without being heated and slamming things around.

When there is conflict, the best way to handle it is by being assertive. Call upon your Spirit team to give you confidence if you're feeling passive aggressive. If you're feeling constantly aggressive, then ask your team to help you in relaxing. Request they assist you in stating your point without hurting, upsetting, or walking over anyone, but with assertive confidence.

During my Film Production days, I was working with a Production Supervisor on a Sony Pictures movie. At times of high stress, she would come off abusive with her staff. Ironically, she wasn't like that with me, but that's usually the case as I have low tolerance for abuse. I naturally have the stance of someone demanding respect that most people give that when I enter a room. I became close with her since I tend to get along well with the extroverted tempestuous difficult types that rub others the wrong way. When I noticed she first stepped out of line with a crew member, I pulled her to the side with calm assertiveness and said, "That was harsh."

She pulled back struck by the statement. Mist glazed over her eyes as she revealed vulnerability. "Was I?" She continued, "I totally respect you. This is why I need you to tell me and smack me into shape if you see me doing that."

Afterwards, when I noticed her slipping into rude, hostile, antagonistic, bullying aggression with a crew member, I'd walk in the room and she'd quickly grow quiet and look at me for validation if she took it too far or not. Soon she began to be cognizant of when she might be crossing the line on her own. It was a proud moment seeing that she wanted to change and become better at dealing with others professionally with assertiveness rather than aggression. It wasn't her intention to be nasty as deep down she is a good giving person, but needed to be taught tools and other effective ways of communicating that wouldn't alienate or turn others off. Unfortunately, spiritual concepts such as this one are not something that is taught in school.

There was one minor incident I recall that happened with a Production Assistant where this woman slammed at him about it just as I happened to be walking into the room again. Minutes later when she was alone with me she asked me if she was too harsh there. I explained that she was and that she can get her point across with greater success by being assertive. People will respect you more and it'll boost morale.

After those instances, I began to notice her softening over the course of the film shoot. She grew to become friendlier, fun, giving, and all smiles with the crew. She was still as much in control and strong as before, but she didn't need to convey that strength through abuse. Before that, she was notoriously known as a mean taskmaster that was whipping the crew into shape as if they were slaves. Others started to mention that they really like this new her. I was proud of watching her shift from aggression to assertiveness in the way that she supervised the crew by the end of the shoot. Sometimes you are in a job or relationship for a reason, which is to allow who you are to rub off on others in a positive way. You might despise your job, but it's not always about you. You may be there to be a positive influence. If human souls kept their ego in check, there would be peace on Earth. No wars, fighting, hate, or causing others pain. It would be as if you were back in Heaven where those negative traits don't exist. Keeping your ego in check is by displaying assertiveness, instead of aggression and passive aggression.

CHAPTER THIRTEEN

*Step Into Your
Soul's Authority*

A guru in India sat on a stage and talked to the audience about someone who was stressed out at their job.

The guru's response was, "Okay, I hope that you get fired from your job."

The guy said, "Oh no, I don't want to get fired."

The guru explained, "You have a job and you're stressed, so I offer to take the job away from you, but now you're stressed about not having a job. It's all in your mind."

Everyone applauds.

How deep would the guru be in the practical world where he would have to hold a 9-6 schedule office job for years with all of the demands that are placed on his back, and all that it entails on his well-being. One reader said that it was easy to wear flowing clothes and sit on a chair on a stage with a turban and dish that out. It's another thing to preach on matters you truly understand because you had to live it and be immersed in it for a long period of time. I take into account all sides to have a greater understanding of the physical reality that different people experience.

On the flip side to counter that the guru had a point, where yes to an extent the misery is in your mind. When you change your perspective to see that not having that job would be far worse than having it, then you lighten up about it and you shift your perspective on it to gratitude and acceptance.

Others may preach about what you need to do, but they may not have lived the kind of life you're undergoing. These can be social media mentors, gurus, or motivational speakers who don't understand why the rest of the world is going through what it's going through. They may not have had to work regular jobs they despise for decades unable to break free. They might not have had to endure child abuse or hardcore toxic addictions. Instead they might have got lucky early on with their self-improvement business.

This is intended to illustrate that sometimes you may be drawn to someone informing you about changing your circumstances, but they have not lived through enough turmoil and darkness to understand the nature of rising above it. It can leave you feeling even more confused and dejected unable to grasp why you're not moving out of a situation you feel stuck in.

Someone told me about a popular speaker lecturing the crowd on getting happy, but they added, "That's easy for her to say, she lives in a $10 million dollar mansion and doesn't have to work a job she can't stand just to survive."

That comment made me ponder on a deeper level growing more aware and observant about each individual's life history. When you're battling with something you have trouble overcoming, you want to hear from someone who lived it rather than some medical doctor who never experienced it. Perhaps the person discussing it has empathy and understanding, or they might have strong psychic spiritual connections that can help, while other times they might have both. If you're seeking healing assistance or motivation, then you'll gravitate towards those that resonate strongly for you. In the end, the intention of all motivators is to motivate you, and if it motivates you to positively change regardless of what that instructor has been through, then they did their job.

As for this particular speaker, she indeed endured a heck of a great deal of trials and tribulations from child sexual abuse to working jobs that sucked out her life force. She had also spent many years putting off the Divine wisdom that was guiding her to make a big change. When she finally did take that step she catapulted to the top of the charts.

Many well-known spiritual and empowerment related speakers and counselors have moved into the role of encouraging people to be optimistic this lifetime. They do an exceptional job reaching an enormous amount people by inspiring and helping them to initiate action that can lead them closer to achieving bliss, growth, and abundance. Every single person on the planet seeking assistance is not drawn to the same teacher or speaker, which is why it's necessary to have a large selection of teachers in this role. One teacher may work for one person, but not for another. They are aligned with communicating in a language or manner that translates best for you.

If you're new to improving your life, then you know when someone's work has assisted you in positively changing it for the better. Some students are inspired to make healthy life changes, some constantly struggle with it, while others give up.

A financially successful motivational speaker who encourages you to be optimistic can be an exceptional motivator. What others have said they take into consideration are two additional major factors associated with a great motivator. One of them is the speaker is financially successful and working for themselves. They have enough income where they work from home full time or wherever they choose. They don't have to slum it day after day forty plus hours a week sitting in traffic to get to and from a soul sucking job they don't care about that is ultimately killing off their life force. It is easier for someone to tell you to get happy when that's the life they already have. How many people struggling in life will be able to tell others to get happy at that point? The energy discord between both is wide and takes some effort to put into practice.

Don't beat yourself up when you experience those periods of frustration, despondence, and pessimism. Be aware of those feelings, make your peace with them, and then begin the process of lifting your spirit back into inspiration and optimism.

Many employees work in harsh or toxic environments that do not promote positive morale or a flexible schedule that allows for abundant productivity. Some are working with a toxic colleague or more, or they are working for a superior that fits that mold. What's worse than that is if they work for both a toxic boss and a toxic colleague. The vibrational distance between being in that space compared to achieving what a financially successful motivating teacher has is super wide to overcome. It is not impossible to do when you see that someone else was able to make that leap and transition. Knowing your motivator was able to do that is an excellent motivation to have in itself.

The financially successful teacher has the life that others dream of, so therefore it's easier for them to be optimistic. They no longer have the restrictions that prohibit them from achieving easy bliss. They're no longer walking in the shoes of someone working a job they despise that is killing off their life force and preventing them from remaining optimistic. We're they this optimistic when they had to slum it in a job they despised in a crummy apartment? It was more than likely a huge struggle for them to get positive in that instant than it is now doing work they love. Even the most wonderful upbeat positive teacher will have some down feeling days too, but you're not seeing that on camera.

The other factor is that some speakers have a naturally sunny disposition. They could have been born bubbly, bouncy, and extroverted with fewer horrid experiences to overcome. These are things such as they're not battling with mental, emotional, or physical disorders, or addictions and abuse that make it challenging everyday to have that award winning bright personality that takes people by storm when they enter a room.

It's challenging to get someone suffering from daily anxiety or depression to shift that energy when they have what some might call a chemical imbalance. Maybe you consume substances that are not great for you thus altering your state of mind to something worse. You take those substances because it gives you a temporary high. Soon that high wears off and you're miserable again until you consume the substance again. This is in order to keep going.

It's easy to sell positive thinking when you're a million-dollar speaker or you work for yourself. I'm sure you would love to meet the 9-6 Monday thru Friday employee who works a job they don't care about for a paycheck and simultaneously pushes perpetual positive thinking. They are rare and some companies are lucky to have that one person in there that brings joy just by being a part of that staff.

Spiritual teachers, speakers, and motivators assist in guiding you in a more enlightened direction, but ultimately you are your own authority. You have the true answers within as to what changes you need to make for yourself to get happy.

I grew up being physically, mentally, spiritually, and emotionally abused by one of my parents. It was repetitive and severe enough that my soul consciousness broke and split apart into numerous selves. I ended up struggling through alcohol, drug, and pill addictions, which also transferred into broken relationships. While things are much better and at peace today than back then, I still struggle to forge forward battling the side effects it brought on at times.

Growing up, I wanted to hear from someone who is or has had to drudge it day after day for decades and eventually escaped that to do what they love full time. Or they were still able to be endlessly optimistic and naturally motivated while working that kind of job. I have never in all my years in the work force encountered someone who was permanently optimistic. Most of them appeared miserable or disappointed in their life.

There are a great many teachers, role models, and motivators threaded around the world with past histories that fit the rags to riches scenario. Those were the inspiring ones I desired to see. They were someone that rose up from the slums of their life to the one they had only envisioned in dreams of Heaven.

Many people look to motivational speakers to inspire them, give them great life tips, or just to hear positive words, but you create your own life. You choose how it will go. If you don't like your life, then take action steps to change it. Pull yourself up by your bootstraps and through faith become your own champion and motivator. If you feel that you can't change it, can't move out of the place you live in, can't leave the job you hate for financial reasons, then you will remain in that position until you take steps to change it.

The odds of winning the lottery jackpot are slim to none, so you can't rely on that, but certainly buying a ticket can increase the rare probability of winning. What you can do is take action steps towards making the life you want a reality. Many people have done it. They've worked jobs they've hated and eventually worked jobs they loved or moved into careers working for themselves.

Working for yourself where you call the shots can have its drawbacks. You still have to answer to yourself and ensure you have consistent income coming in so you can pay your bills. Prayer and positive affirmations help alter your perception, but it still needs to be coupled with action since it is rare that anything magnificent will land in your lap with no effort. Even just a little effort goes a long way as it gets that energy moving in that direction.

While many will talk about how you have to be happy first and then the abundance will come, it's easy to say that when you have the abundance, therefore it's not always entirely true. The reality is there are many miserable people that achieved financial abundance in their lifetime and were still miserable afterwards.

Be as optimistic as you can be in general, since no one is rubbed the right way being around a miserable grump, but it certainly won't play that big of a part in preventing what you want from coming to you. People that achieved what they wanted regardless of being miserable or optimistic is because they worked hard and went after it without stopping. It's hard work and persistence that helps you achieve. It's not giving up no matter how many setbacks or roadblocks get in your way. It is rising into your Divine soul power of fearless assertive confidence.

It's also more than practicing positive thinking and bliss in hopes of achieving the ultimate reward, which are abundance and endless blessings. Don't be mistaken by this message telling you to think negatively instead. By all means, positive thinking is always the way to go, but in the most efficient way. You cannot deny how you're feeling by masking it with false positive thinking in order to convince you that you are positive, when deep down you are miserable. You are miserable with where your life is at, miserable that you don't have a lover, miserable that you're not doing work that you love, miserable that your life is not where you thought it would be, and miserable because you feel perpetually stuck. Those are valid feelings that need to be addressed and dealt with one at a time. You can choose to be miserable for a lifetime that the lover did not come, or you can make the most of it and accept it by letting it go.

The problem with saying that positive thinking is not the way to go is that it confuses one by glorifying negative thinking. It's basically saying, "Hey, it's okay to be miserable. If that's how you feel, then let it out and be proud of that."

That's dangerous to say since people are miserable and negative enough. No one has any problem being negative. It takes work to be positive, but the positive feeling has to be experienced naturally. If it's forced, then it's still negative with a false layer of optimism.

Numerous studies revealed surprising revelations that successful business entrepreneur millionaires were those who had a tough time in school. They might not have gone to College, but might have graduated from High School with a B or C average and sometimes lower. Most were not "A" students with a 4.0 GPA. I remember before my days in the Entertainment Industry that in the 1980's it was known that bigwig producers would make someone with a College Degree serve coffee just to prove that in the end it doesn't matter to them.

This isn't justifying or discrediting school achievers, nor is it attempting to sway anyone from striving to be your best in school. This is illustrating to those who have struggled not to give up. Don't believe you won't amount to anything because you did poorly in school or didn't receive a degree. There are numerous examples of people who did poorly in school, came from a poor or middle class background, yet ended up becoming millionaires. This is partially because they tried harder, while conveying passion and dedication. They used more mental prowess to succeed despite not having a degree or a high GPA. They were optimistic, persistent, and streets smart.

A top CEO of a well-known real estate franchise

informed me that she never went to College, but instead received her degree at the "school of hard knocks". Her offices combined bring in over $150 million in real estate revenue. Not bad for someone who came from nothing, didn't do well in school, and with little education.

Everyone entertains doubts or negative thinking at some point, including the most evolved enlightened being. It is humanely impossible for one person to be 100% positive in thinking every second of their life. Earth is not Heaven, and doubts and negative thinking will creep up even with the most positive appearing person. If you think positive, then you will achieve blessings and rewards. This is not always true and can put someone into a dangerous predicament. The secret to achieving blessings is a combination of factors that include taking action as well as being optimistic that you can do it. You can't layer your negative thoughts with positive thinking. This is like taking a pill to numb emotional pain. It may numb those rough edges, but it doesn't get rid of the issues unless it's addressed and dealt with in order to heal and then release it. Then you have a clean slate to forge forward fearlessly.

CHAPTER FOURTEEN

Fearless Assertive
Confident Soul

Show your best self by becoming a fearless confident soul that walks in faith. Share your light with others whenever you can. Let it out and let it shine bright. This inspires a mighty movement of peace. The hardness and toxicity that has plagued humankind for so long is outdated. The light inside you must be allowed to breath freely. Allow it to shine outwardly by taking back the control of your surroundings. Be a warrior of light and do your best to stay in that space even when you stumble upon a roadblock or a difficult person. Demanding people are merely acting out from their ego, which has no power or validity with anything real or long lasting. The ego lives in fear and acts out in fits of temper much like a child having an outburst when it doesn't get what it wants. You find peace, joy, strength and love when you remain centered in the light.

When you lose your way, ask for heavenly assistance to get back on track. The more you ask for help and work with your Spirit team to reach this space of contentment, then the easier it gets. What can work for you might be lighting a candle and meditating on this light. Call in your Spirit team to begin the process of re-aligning your soul back into confidence. Empty out your negative thoughts as you focus on this candlelight. Close your eyes and envision that the flame of the light is taking over any negative thoughts and blasting it away while lifting it off your body. Make room in your consciousness to receive the messages coming in from Spirit to help you be at peace and feel encompassed by love.

I have crossed paths with a wide variety of people with different belief systems and values. I have witnessed those who might disagree with any of this or who find it to be ineffective. Yet, these are the same people that struggle in a constant uphill battle. Or they might be the ones who have been stagnant with no hope for escape. When in those states your ego dominates your life big time ensuring that you never progress.

Within you is the knowledge of all lifetimes. Within you is the knowledge of why you are here. Pay attention to your intuition as that is one of the many barometer gauges that exist within your soul that accurately receives heavenly messages. All human souls receive heavenly communication everyday without exception. It is irrelevant what the soul's personal values and beliefs are, and whether they're aware that it is indeed their Guides and Angels. Pay attention to the messages in order to help you navigate through life much easier than if you were not aware of them.

Keeping your vibration high takes daily work. It's a lifestyle and view change you're adopting. One day you are riding on cloud nine with joy, which raises your vibration. Your vibration remains high until a negative thought enters your mind thus causing it to take a dip again. The next day you go on a drinking binge. This drinking binge prompts your vibration to drop astronomically. It can be a struggle to raise it than it is to drop it. Raising it back up can feel like pushing a huge boulder up a steep hill. Those privy to this knowledge can raise their vibration much easier than someone unaware of what to do in order to get it there. Having an interfering culprit like the ego is what gets its kicks out of double-crossing you and ensuring your vibration stays low. It makes sure that you do not succeed. When you make a commitment to incorporating higher vibration methods into your life every day, then you will notice the changes in your life shifting in a more positive direction.

It's easy to lose sight of why you're here. The way human life has been set up and structured by the ego in others has caused enormous discontent.

Human ego trained others to be unhappy and glum by thriving for nonsense. Not everyone is affected by the harsh energies of the planet. These people have made adjustments to their lifestyle choices. This includes living in areas of nature with little to no chaos and people. Watching what they ingest in their physical bodies and taking care of it through daily exercise. They ensure the people they surround themselves with are high vibrational. They avoid the negativities of social media, the internet, and gossip entertainment.

There are a great many positives to Earthly life. People took what they innately learned from the spirit world and built homes, created work and jobs for others, designed transportation, as well as an ease of communication through advanced technological devices. These are some of the fantastic concrete practical necessities for human life. These are practical ways of surviving on a planet that is spilling over the edges.

However, interpersonal relationships continue to suffer sliding rapidly on a decline. Love is lacking, while cruelty and unfriendliness is gaining steam. It is true that human souls manage to find the love when a crises hits. They intervene when they notice someone is being pushed down, but the love they exude in those instances is temporary. You grow lost in the nonsense of the noise of the ego. Some are consumed by jobs they're not happy in, or you're living check-to-check, or struggling to find work. Perhaps you're in relationships that are unsatisfying, or you're perpetually single longing for a long-term committed love relationship that never surfaces. You're forced to be in situations you do not want to be in. What an effort it is to get to a place of feeling eternally happy.

When you're faced with circumstances that do not jive with your higher self, examine how you arrived at that place. Look at the underlying cause that has prompted you to feel negative when this happens. Identify it and then dig deep into understanding why it has upset you. There are circumstances that no doubt have made you angry or prompted feelings of discomfort. Maybe you ran into someone at the store who was rude to you. You being a sensitive absorbed that like nobody's business. It ends up putting you in a funk for the rest of the day. For some sensitive's, they'll be angry for a minute, others for hours, or you could be one of those who immerses in the energy for the rest of the day. Avoid beating yourself up over it. It just means that you're a hyper sensitive psychic sponge. You have compassion and love within you as all souls do, even though this might be difficult to grasp.

Whenever you witness ugliness in someone else, remember that they were born with the deepest love and compassion beyond measure. What you're observing with them is the darkness of ego at its worst. This soul has given its power away to the Darkness, their lower self, and ego. The ego cannot be reasoned with or convinced of anything, but of what it wants. The ego seeks to sabotage themselves or others. It can be someone who slanders someone they don't care for. A high vibrational soul that is not pleased with something does not waste its time resorting to negativity or in giving it any attention. It only focuses on the things it enjoys.

When you witness aggression or disrespectful behavior flying at you, then you will absorb that energy. It seeps into your aura and soul. It causes an array of negative circumstances and moods to assault you. Find positive exercises that can assist you in releasing it and letting that go. It might feel easier said than done, but when a slight happens in your world, your ego has trouble letting go of it. When you understand this concept of separating yourself from the troublesome ego, it becomes simpler to manage and temper it.

When you have a higher degree of sensitivity than other souls, then you are more likely to be affected by someone else's ego. You're a psychic sponge who easily absorbs the negative or off putting energies in others. It is a gift, but at times it can feel like a curse when you enter environments with people that display low vibrational behavioral patterns. You absorb that negative energy which drops your mood affecting your inner and outer world.

When you grow negative, moody, or agitated, then this is a sign of two possible conclusions. One is that you've ingested low vibrational foods or drinks. Or you may have absorbed this energy from someone toxic you crossed paths with. It can be a stranger on the sidewalk who walked passed you. If they're displaying low vibrational behavior, then that energy is lodged in their aura. As a tuned in sensitive psychic sponge, you've absorbed that into your aura sometimes without knowing it. The super tuned in psychic sponges are typically aware they just absorbed this energy from someone in passing.

The souls you absorbed this energy from do not always intend to have a low vibration. It's usually done innocently and naively, or sometimes in other words not knowing any better. Some souls have not evolved enough to be more in tune to something outside of themselves. This is partially why that particular soul is living an Earthly life.

Those in tune with the Other Side, the soul and spirit, are turned off by harsh people and energies. They steer clear of those that perpetually display low vibrational traits. This can be from the guy trying to pull a fast one by nickel and diming someone to buy a car. We call them pushy salespeople. They don't care about you, but what's in your wallet. On the flipside, they have a quota and if they want to keep that particular job, they know they need to do whatever it takes to sell a car. There are easygoing salespeople who do care about you and do not display shark attack like behavior. They don't attempt to find ways to sell you something when you're having doubts or feeling uncomfortable about it. This type of salesperson will simply say, "I'm here to answer any questions you have about any of this. If you're interested, then let me know."

It can be your employer or someone you work with who puts on the fakeness whenever you enter the room. As a tuned in soul you can sense them a mile away. They're threatened by your higher frequency energy. They subconsciously know that you're on to them. This also turns off a lower vibrational energy in someone else. Low vibrational human souls are threatened by someone that exudes a high confident vibrational energy. The low vibrational soul's ego feels out of your league. High vibrational people don't feel threatened by others unless that person is exuding negative energy traits. They're not threatened but repulsed. Sometimes it can also be that you and these other people you come into contact with don't know each other well enough to accept your differences.

There was another incident in my former film days where I was working for an employer who rubbed everyone the wrong way. I noticed others kept coming to me here and there to express how this woman upsets them. This wasn't the same woman in the earlier story. There was one day when someone pointed out to me something negative about her.

I responded, "Yeah, I'm hearing that quite a bit. It's best to ignore it."

They said, "I guess that's all one can do."

That banter got me thinking about this woman. I decided to make a pact to meet her half way where I would throw on the charm and friendliness. The next day I went into her office unannounced and sat in her guest chair. She was all business asking if there was something I needed.

I said, "No, I'm just visiting. Wanted to say hi and see how you're doing."

She seemed a little stunned as if no one had

bothered to do that before. Although the business armor and cold reserve was still up, I noticed she flinched and softened slightly allowing just a little bit of light out. She attempted to engage with me and make some small talk. For me personally this was an effort since I dislike small talk. Something miraculous soon happened where we started this lighthearted dialogue banter.

The next day I continued with the new pact to visit her and to get to know her more. I proceeded to do that every day realizing we were bonding and hitting it off. Soon it was no longer an effort for me to chill with her briefly or for her to engage. Both of our reserves were coming down. Once I tore down those walls and met her half way, not only did the morale within the production company improve, but our connection improved as well. We were not just two cold ice conquerors going toe to toe. She started to open up a little bit more as time went by.

To make a long story short at the time of this writing, I've known her personally for over two decades now. Like many of the friendships I made throughout the business, we continue to talk and meet up for the occasional get together. She's a wonderful soul with an amazing generous heart. When others have asked how I met her, I go back into time and remember that it didn't start off that way. Sometimes when you take the time to know someone who has the cold reserve up, you discover they're not as hostile as they are coming off. It's human nature to instantly judge someone who hasn't spoken a word instead of diving into who they are.

This coldness and reserve has grown in others thanks to the technological age. Newer and future generations are being raised on devices that train you to be lacking in honest face-to-face soul connections. For those that have gone out on a date you've probably noticed some of the typical preliminary questions. They want to know what your job is or what kind of work do you do. What kind of car do you drive? These ego driven questions are externally based. Your job does not define you in real reality, but the human ego has set their life up in a way that their whole world revolves around what kind of job you do. Who cares what you do for a living. Unless you're working in a field that is your passion and it brings you joy, then it is irrelevant what kind of work you do. This passion is your life purpose, but many do not work in jobs that are their passion. For most people it is a paycheck that squeezes the life force out of that soul. They're usually under stress and grumbling about life in general.

When you absorb the ions of negative and cold energy around you, then this can put a damper on your spirit until you address it. You can sit around and hope that something amazing will happen around you that will suddenly raise your vibration, or you can address it and do something about it immediately. It can be going for a walk in a nature setting. This is followed by taking deep healthy breathes in and requesting that your spirit team release any and all negative energy that has latched onto your soul. It can be getting together with an optimistic friend who observes healthy life choices. It can be someone that lifts your aura just by being in your vicinity. You can throw on a funny movie or make love to your relationship partner. What you're trying to do is re-raise your vibration. Taking basic soul enhancing steps when an assault has attacked your aura can do the trick.

CHAPTER FIFTEEN

Live Your Life Be Free

Everyone has experienced some hard times at one time or another. You might have negative things to say about it. The ego fixates on the horrid that came out of something rather than the positive gained. Rise above your ego and ask yourself, "What greatness did my soul consciousness receive out of that experience? What was awesome about it?"

The soul's experiences happen for a reason regardless if they're challenging or not. It is not because you did something to deserve it, but because your soul is destined for greatness. It reaches those heights of greatness through the challenges. You're here in this Earthly life school to find ways that suit you in order to enhance your soul and spirit. You're not here to find out what the latest sale on jeans is or rip through relationships selfishly with no care in the world. In order to improve you have much to gain. When something negative happens in your world, work on looking at it from an optimistic perspective.

An exercise you can do is to pick up a journal or a notebook. Use that notepad as your diary to put in only optimistic viewpoints in your life. When you find that you're buried heavily in negative thoughts and emotions unable to break away, take a moment to pull the notebook out. Devote a page or more to whatever it is that is upsetting you. If it's a person you know, then write that person's name in your journal entry. Instead of focusing on what they did to upset you or whatever circumstance has upset you, shift that into something positive. Think about all of the qualities you love about the person that has angered you. Remove your ego from the equation and look at that person through the eyes of an egoless angel. How would they see that person's soul within? List everything that is positive about them and how that affects you in an optimistic way. I know some may grumble when reading that and believe me I understand. I have an ego too! When someone has hurt or angered you it's going to be difficult to see them through the eyes of love. Know that when you're looking at them through the eyes of love, you're not condoning their behavior and nor do you have to remain buddies with them. You're doing this exercise as a release. It's for your benefit in order to remove that old, tired, angry energy you're carrying around that surrounds the person or circumstance. You do not need that energy, but in order to release it, acknowledging it with love is what raises your vibration. When your vibration is raised you are more apt to receiving clearer communication from the spirit world, which in turn assists you on your path towards abundance in all forms. It is what feeds this fearless assertive confidence into your spirit.

Your mind may begin to wander to all of the things you feel this person (or circumstance) has done that has hurt or upset you. However, you will not write those things down. Remember this is a positive journal. You will immediately adjust your thoughts back to the positive things about this person. Let's say it was an ex-lover who cheated on you, was abusive, or left you and the relationship. You will not write any of those things down, but rather will focus on their good qualities. If you're only able to come up with one good quality, then write that one down. It is an exercise that takes much effort in this case, because you're holding anger towards this person for doing one or all of the things I suggested. Your ego refuses to see the goodness in someone who has upset or hurt you, which is understandable, but we're working on letting it go here.

If it is a circumstance that happened to cause you upset, then you will write down in this journal the optimistic features that have come out of that. For example, you receive a traffic ticket. Instead of focusing heavily on how you have no time to take care of the ticket, or no money to pay for it, write

195

down the positive benefits that you've gained from the ticket. You might write something down like: "This has taught me to drive more carefully."

That statement feels far better than saying, "I have no money. How am I going to pay for this! It wasn't even my fault!"

The ticket could've been a karmic thread reaction to another issue going on in your life that needs addressing. Usually there is a domino effect of events that are within the same energy vibration.

This exercise may not immediately change your life, but it will gradually guide you into positively taking steps in changing your life. It will assist you in getting into the habit of bouncing back from upsetting situations much more quickly than you normally would. It will help you to view circumstances and people in a more positive light. The key is if you're going to play this game, then you have to play objectively. Putting all things positive and optimistic in this journal is the exercise. Only write your blessings, appreciations and gratitude for situations and people in your life. This absolutely includes everything and everyone that causes you to feel negative emotions. This might be challenging, but in the end it will be rewarding as you are re-training your mind to think positively. This raises your vibration in the process, which assists with attracting in positive circumstances and people to you over the course of time. Because it raises your vibration it also clears out the debris that accumulates in and around the communication line to Heaven and your Spirit team. If it doesn't do anything, but allow you to start shining your true loving light, then that is all that matters in the end.

The higher self is a problem solver, but the darkness of ego is a wretched problem seeker. It might appear to be louder than your higher self and your Spirit team of guides and angels. This is due to a couple of factors. The atmosphere of the Earth plane is extremely thick and dense that connecting to the Other Side through all of the toxic debris makes it challenging. Your guides and angels are louder and more powerful than any ego. Yet, when the soul is in the Earth dimension, the communication lines are heavier and dirtier. The ego easily rises through the dirt. It rises as soon as your soul enters into this human life. The ego is activated in a big way. When the soul is in the earth plane it's like roaming through life with ear plugs and blindfolds on. Anyone who has put on a blindfold and ear plugs to sleep at night may point out how they can sometimes faintly hear light sounds with them on. The higher self strains to hear Heaven through this muffled sound. When a human soul lives in a higher vibrational state, this allows light in, which gives rise to the higher self. Suddenly that soul is hearing their guides and angels more clearly than usual.

You are not alone as you are surrounded by at least one Spirit Guide and one Guardian Angel from your human birth until human death. They assist you down the right path in order to fulfill your purpose while here. When you are in your higher self's state you connect with your Spirit team on the other side with greater efficiency. When you are in your lower self's state or ego, then you block heavenly guidance and messages that keep you on the right path and assist you in achieving your desires. In my connections with Heaven, I've discovered that all are loved and seen through the eyes of love. Do your best to keep the darkness of your ego in check and exude love full time.

This is your life and you need to live it confidently for you. Let no one shatter your dreams, feel no guilt about who you are, and apologize to no one about your gifts and talents. Don't allow what other people say to tell you're not qualified for something if it's something you're passionate about inside. You're not here to live the way the critics around want you to live. Can you imagine taking what other people say to heart? You would never accomplish anything. God's sends His best here, which means He knows you are great enough to stomp out that darkness in other people and follow your Divine calling. He knows you are strong enough to withstand the forces of dark critics by ignoring it and forging forward and eyes ahead on what He's calling you to do. It's no one's business how you choose to live your life. You may feel indebted to certain people in your circle this lifetime, but in higher truth the only soul you are beholden to is your own and your Divine contract.

Live your life freely by confidently going after what you desire with passion, enjoyment, and enthusiasm. Life may have dealt you a challenging hand, but use that to your advantage. Challenges are not intended to punish you, but to strengthen you into a warrior. Take the hint and toughen up.

Don't allow setbacks to keep you down. When you trip, stumble, and fall, then rise back up again ready to forge on into battle. Revert to faith by leaning on God and the Angels for strength, confidence building, and support.

Fight for your life! If there is something irking you about a decision or purchase or commitment made - then don't hesitate to taking action or feeling guilty about canceling or deleting it from your life. If a situation is leaving you to feel taken advantage of, then take steps to fix it.

Acquire knowledge and wisdom through the process of living and feeling good about how your life trajectory ends up. Make the decision to change your ships course and aim your soul towards the direction of your dreams. The things you say and do now set in motion what is to come six months to a year from that point, so be aware and conscious of what it is you are putting out into the Universe.

Take the occasional step back to retreat and take stock in how your life has gone to date. Notice all of what you've accomplished. Examine your triumphs, your sorrows, your successes, and your challenges. What was lost and what was gained? Look forward to the next six months of your life and affirm that it will go with superior promise. You will do your best to ensure that it will be even better than it's ever been.

Every morning you wake up, have gratitude for what you have now, then mentally say to your consciousness that you will make today count.

One exercise can be to find an empty jar or

canister, get a stack of post-its or little notes, and leave those blank notes next to the jar. At least once a week write at least one awesome thing that happened for you that week or each day. Even if it was someone who showered you with a smile that stuck. Fold up the little note and put it in the jar. Every several months or so often pull all of the little notes out and read each one and notice the blessings and good things that actually did take place in your life that you might have normally brushed off. Some people focus only on lack or what went wrong, but one rarely shines light on all of the good that took place. Focusing on the good expands that energy into more good things.

Focus on the good that happens in your life that might seem miniscule because it's not the big lottery financial win. If you get a flat tire that ruined your day, don't talk about that aspect of it on the post-it, but instead mention who intervened to help your day brighten up, including if it was the tow truck driver that got you up and running again. There are blessings all around you when you take the time to notice them.

Derive pleasure out of the day with the things you love the most. Don't allow any stress or negativity to override this pleasure. This also means avoid engaging in anything that's going to bring you misery. Focus on the good and the uplifting. Go after what you want without reservation. The happier you allow yourself to become, then the healthier you turn out to be. This equates to a longer more fulfilling, passionate, joyous life. This is what every soul wants and deserves, but it takes a bit of effort on your part to re-train your mind into manifesting that fearless assertive confidence within you.

Incorporate regular bouts of fun times, make and connect with friends, family, and acquaintances. Open up and be sociable with others without any demands. Connecting with others through lightheartedness gives you a joy boost, which then raises your vibration. A high vibration is what brings positive manifestations into your life. Being sociable has added health benefits including that of being a wonderful stress reliever. This version of sociability with others does not mean resorting to gossip, slander, and complaints, but rather choosing to enjoyably engage with other people's energies. Seek out camaraderie, community, and positive shifts. Open up your heart to others with love and affection. Taking care of your well-being from the body, mind, and your soul are important because it is your temple and vessel that you have been given for the sake of numerous purposes. You have to take of all parts of you and take that seriously. You are loved even when you doubt it, avoid it, shun it and do everything in your power to deny it. When you reach that threshold of completing your run, the only thing you take with you is love. If you gain any knowledge of value, remember to love more, give more, and have compassion no matter how unpopular it's become. Only then can you truly discover that magic your soul secretly desires.

If God raised you, then you would grow up to see the love in all souls. You would exude love and joy full time. The best parts of you are what God is, and the worst parts are the darkness of your ego.

Practice with starting each day on a high note, since that will set the tone for the next twenty-four hours. How often have you woken up in a negative mood only to find that's carried into the rest of the day? Your coffee machine won't work, you're running late for work, and discover the traffic is worse than it's ever been. You walk into work and thrown at you are one issue after another. By the time you get out of work agitated, you race home to have a drink. It take a great deal of effort to shift your vibrational energy back into confidence, but the tools to do so are already within you.

Rejoice, celebrate, and love all that you are inside and out. You are perfect and beautiful through the eyes of God and the angels. This love for your soul is unconditional. See yourself in this same light as Heaven sees you and remember to practice self-care. You are intended for greatness. If you never do anything else, but let your loving light shine through to the world, then that will be enough to help combat all the evil in the world.

Your life moves in cycles that fluctuate. You can detect when an official cycle is ending due to all of the back to back closing of doors that appears to be happening. This can cause you to be filled with enormous tension. Allow the doors that need to be closed to do so as it is prepping you for a new chapter. You can use that time spent retreating, laying low, gathering knowledge, purging, and centering, so that you may rise in strength with clarity for your next new chapter.

Personal changes are much like the cycles of the weather seasons that ebb and flow. You are moving through a series of chapters, peaks, and valleys every day. Those are great times to evaluate and probe deeper into what you've experienced to date, how you've grown, what you've learned, and how you'll choose to move forward. What will you leave behind and what will you take with you on the next part of your soul's journey onward and upward into Utopia and beyond?

Acknowledgments

Thank you to God, my Spirit Team Council, and to all of the loyal readers that have hopped on this awesome train ride of mine and stayed on. I am forever blessed and grateful for your eternal support of the work we do. Thank you also for supporting the arts and the artists of the world.

ALSO BY KEVIN HUNTER

Stay Centered Psychic Warrior
Warrior of Light
Empowering Spirit Wisdom
Darkness of Ego
Realm of the Wise One
Transcending Utopia
Reaching for the Warrior Within
Spirit Guides and Angels
Soul Mates and Twin Flames
Raising Your Vibration
Divine Messages for Humanity
Connecting with the Archangels
Monsters and Angels
The Seven Deadly Sins
Love Party of One
Twin Flame Soul Connections
A Beginner's Guide to the Four Psychic Clair Senses
Tarot Card Meanings
Attracting in Abundance
Abundance Enlightenment
Living for the Weekend
Ignite Your Inner Life Force
Awaken Your Creative Spirit
The Essential Kevin Hunter Collection
Metaphysical Divine Wisdom (Series)

STAY CENTERED PSYCHIC WARRIOR
A Psychic Medium's Trip Through the Darkness and Light of the
Spirit Worlds, and Other Paranormal Phenomena

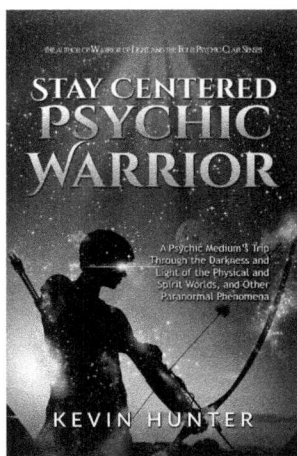

In *Stay Centered Psychic Warrior*, metaphysical teacher, psychic, medium, and author, Kevin Hunter talks about what it's like battling between mental health issues and the deeply potent psychic input that continuously falls into his soul's consciousness throughout each day. He offers plenty of examples and discussions of his brushes with spirit, seeing and hearing the dead, the power of the Darkness and the Light in both the physical and spirit worlds, along with sharing his numerous personal psychic and mediumship essays, glimpses of the Other Side, near death experiences, past lives, soul contracts, traveling to and from the Spirit Worlds, spirit guides and angels, recognizing your own psychic gifts, and much more!

This unique autobiography focuses on psychic and mediumship related content coupled with the soul's journey and purpose. Stay Centered Psychic Warrior is an intensely forceful and revealing read that doesn't shy away from the uncomfortable, the Darkness, abuse, mental health issues, while uplifting it with the many blessings of the Light and intriguing day to day psychic phenomena all in one. Allow it to inspire you to recognize your own psychic gifts knowing there is much more to this Earthly life than can be seen or comprehended. Be empowered to break through the rubble and stand strong and centered under the powerful Light that shines through any Darkness.

A Beginner's Guide to the
FOUR PSYCHIC CLAIR SENSES

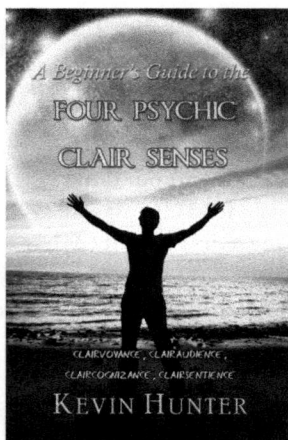

Many believe psychic gifts are bestowed upon select chosen ones, while others don't believe in the craft at all. The reality is every soul is born with heightened psychic gifts and capabilities, but somewhere along the way those senses have dimmed. All are capable of being a conduit with the other side, including those closed off and blocked to it. There are a variety of enlightened beings residing in the spirit realms to assist human souls that request their help. They use varying means and methods to communicate with you called clair channels. These clairs are crystal clear etheric senses used to communicate with any higher being, spirit guide, angel, departed loved one, archangel, and God.

The *Four Psychic Clair Senses* illustrates what the core senses are, examples of how the author picks up on messages, how you can recognize the guidance, and other fun metaphysical psychic stuff. You are a walking divination tool that allows you to communicate with Spirit. The clairs enable you to receive heavenly messages, guidance, and information that positively assist you or another along your Earthly journey. Read about the four core clairs in order to pinpoint what best describes you and how to have a better understanding of what they are and how they work for you.

TAROT CARD MEANINGS

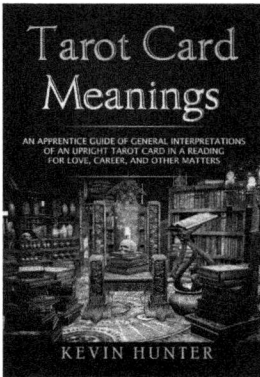

Tarot Card Meanings is an encyclopedia reference guide that takes the Tarot apprentice reader through each of the 78 Tarot Cards offering the potential general meanings and interpretations that could be applied when conducting a reading. The meanings included can be applied to most anything whether it be spiritual, love, general, or work related questions.

Many novices struggle with reading the Tarot as they want to know what a card can mean in their readings. They grow stuck staring at three cards side by side and having no idea what it could be telling them. The Tarot Card Meanings book can assist by pointing you in the general direction of where to look. It will not give you the ultimate answers and should not be taken verbatim, as that is up to you as the reader to come to that conclusion. The more you practice, read, and study the Tarot, then the better you become.

Tarot Card Meanings avoids diving into the Tarot history, or card spreads and symbolism, but instead focuses solely on the potential meaning of a card in a general, love, or work reading. This gives you a structure to jump off of, but it is up to you to take that energy and add the additional layers to your reading, while trusting your higher self, intuition, instincts and Spirit team's guidance and messages. Anything included in the Tarot Card Meanings book is an overview and not intended to be gospel. It is merely one suggested version of the potential meanings of each of the 78 Tarot cards in a reading. It may assist the novice that is having trouble interpreting cards for themselves.

ALSO AVAILABLE BY KEVIN HUNTER

Books that Empower, Enlighten, Educate, and Entertain!

Just as your body needs physical food to survive,
your soul needs spiritual food for well-being nourishment.

THE ESSENTIAL KEVIN HUNTER COLLECTION

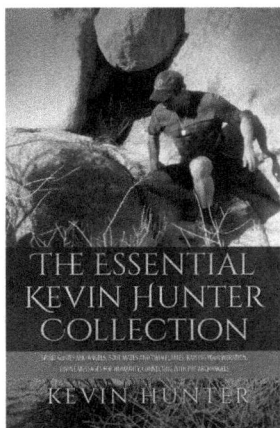

Kevin Hunter an empowering author specializing in a variety of genres, but he is most notably known for his work in the realms of spirituality, metaphysical, and self-help. He has assisted people around the world with standing in their power, and in having a stronger connection with Heaven, while navigating the materialistic practical world. Now some of his popular spiritually based books are available in this one gigantic volume.

The Essential Kevin Hunter Collection is the spiritual bible that contains over 500 pages of content geared towards improving and enhancing your life. It is for those who prefer to have

everything in one gigantic book. The content included in this edition are from the books: *Spirit Guides and Angels, Soul Mates and Twin Flames, Raising Your Vibration, Divine Messages for Humanity, Connecting with the Archangels, Warrior of Light, Empowering Spirit Wisdom, and Darkness of Ego.*

211

TRANSCENDING UTOPIA
Reopening the Pathway to Divinity

Transcending Utopia is packed with practical and spirit knowledge that focuses on enhancing your life through empowering divinely guided spiritual related teachings, inspiration, wisdom, guidance, and messages. The way to accelerate existence on Earth towards Utopia is if every person on the planet resided in their soul's true nature, which is in a state of all love, joy, and peace. The ultimate Nirvana is surpassing that perfection through methods that a limited consciousness could ever dream possible. This is the exceptional glory your soul was born into before the dense turbulence of Earthly life enveloped and suffocated you.

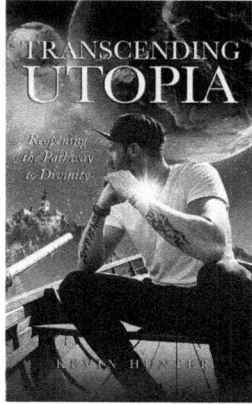

Transcending Utopia is to go beyond your limits and travel outside of the generic mundane materialistic achievement that human beings taught one another to thrive for. A utopian society is where everything is perfectly blissful on all levels according to the sanctified values you were born with. The sensations connected to how flawless everything feels in that moment reveals the authentic perfection you were made from. Utopia is the ideal paradise as imagined in one's dreams that seems to be inaccessible by human standards. It is a state of mind that is possible to reach by adopting broader ways of looking at circumstances while being disciplined about how you conduct your life. You search for a sign of this utopia through external means, only to be consistently left with disappointment. This is because utopia begins and ends inside the spark that burns within your spirit like a pilot light waiting to be ignited.

LIVING FOR THE WEEKEND
The Winding Road Towards Balancing
Career Work and Spiritual Life

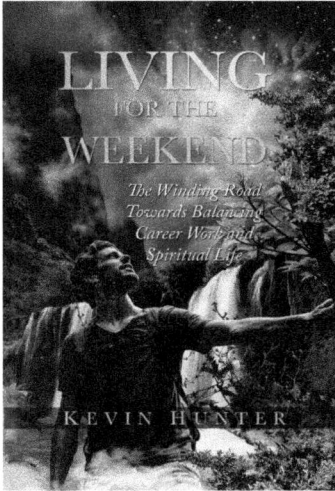

Working hard to ensure your bills are paid can leave your soul spiritually starved for soul nourishment. When your ultimate goal is to obtain enough money to be comfortable that you become carried away in that current, then there is little to no room for Divine enrichment.

Many work to survive in jobs they hate because it's the way it is. As a result, they experience and endure all sorts of emotional pain whether it is through depression, sadness, anger, or any other kind of negative stressor. Some silently suffer through this emotional strain gradually killing off their life force. If you don't have a healthy social life and positive fun filled activities and hobbies to balance that burden outside of that, then that could add additional tension. What's it all for if you can't live the life you've always wanted to live? Instead, you spend your days growing forever miserable and broken.

Living for the Weekend examines the pitfalls, struggles, as well as the benefits available in the current modern day working world. This is followed up with spiritual and practical tips, guidance, messages, and discussions on ways to incorporate more balance and enlightenment to a cutthroat material driven world.

213

Attracting in Abundance
Opening the Divine Gates to Inviting in Blessings and Prosperity Through Body, Mind, and Soul Spirit

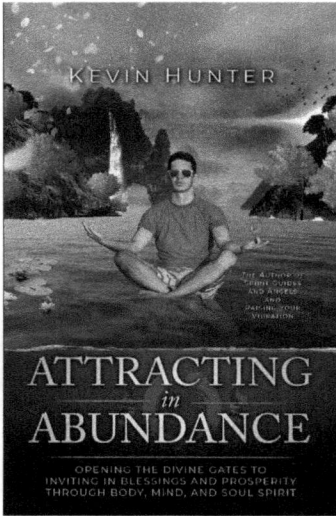

Having enough money to survive comfortably enough on this physical plane is part of obtaining abundance, but it's not the destination and purpose to thrive for. You could work hard to make enough money to the point you are set for life, but that won't necessarily equate to happiness. Achieving a content satisfied state of joy and serenity starts with examining your soul's state and overall well-being. When that's in place, then the rest will follow.

Attracting in Abundance combines practical and spirit wisdom surrounding the nature of abundance. This is something that most everyone can get on board with because all human beings desire physical comforts, blessings, and prosperity, regardless of their personal values and belief systems. *Attracting in Abundance* is broken up into three parts to help move you towards inviting abundance into your life on all levels. "Part One" contains some no-nonsense lectures surrounding the philosophies, concepts, and debates on the laws of attracting in abundance. "Part Two" is the largest of the sections geared towards fine tuning the soul into preparing for abundance. "Part Three" is the final lesson plan to help crack open the gates of abundance with various helpful tidbits, guidance, and messages as well as the blocks that can prevent abundance from coming in.

The B-Side to the Attracting in Abundance book

ABUNDANCE ENLIGHTENMENT
*An Easy Motivational Guide to
the Laws of Attracting in Abundance
and Transforming Your Soul*

Ultimate authentic success surrounds your soul's growth and evolving process. It's when you realize that none of the physical ego driven desires matter in the end. You can work hard to make sure you stay afloat, you're able to pay your bills, and support yourself and family, but you're not chasing popularity for external validation. Any amount of goodness displayed from your heart is the true measure of real accomplishment.

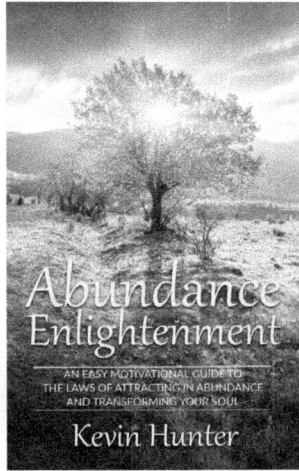

An overflowing feeling of optimism and love coupled with faith and action is what increases the chances of attracting good things and positive experiences to you. Abundance is more than monetary and financial increase. It can also be about reaching an optimistic well-being state of joy, peace, and love. This positive emotional mindful state simultaneously attracts in blessings.

Abundance Enlightenment is the follow up book to *Attracting in Abundance*. It contains both practical guidance and spirit wisdom that can be applied to everyday life. Some of the key topics surround the laws of attraction as well as healthier money management and improving your soul to help make you a fine tuned in abundance attractor.

MONSTERS AND ANGELS
*An Empath's Guide to Finding Peace in a Technologically Driven
World Ripe with Toxic Monsters and Energy Draining Vampires*

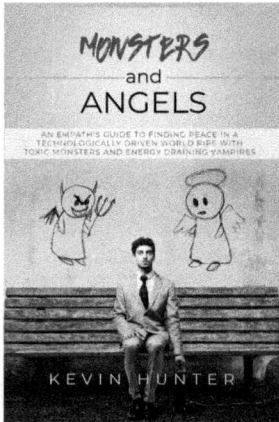

Every person on the planet is capable of being empathic and sensitive, to becoming an energy vampire or toxic monster. No one is exempt from displaying the darker sides of their ego. The easiest and most efficient way to spread any kind of energy is online. Every time you log onto the Internet, there is a larger chance you're going to see something related to the news, media, or gossip areas thrown in front of you, even if you attempt to

avoid it as much as possible. You're absorbing everything that your consciousness faces, including the ugly and the wicked, which has its own consequences. This tempestuous energy is tossed into the Universe ultimately creating a flame-throwing battleground inside and around you.

Monsters and Angels discusses how technology, media, and social media have an immense power in distributing both positive and negative influences far and wide. This is about being mindful of what can negatively affect your state of being, and how to counter and avoid that when and wherever possible. This is why it's beneficial to govern yourself, your life, and your surroundings like a strict disciplined executive.

TWIN FLAME SOUL CONNECTIONS
*Recognizing the Split Apart, the Truths and Myths of Twin Flames,
Soul Love Connections, Soul Mates, and Karmic Relationships*

Twin Flames have a shared ongoing sentiment and quest from the moment they're a spark shooting out of God's love that explodes into a blinding white fire that breaks apart causing one to be two, until two become one again, separate and whole, and back around again. Looking into the eyes of your Twin Flame is like looking into the eyes of God, because to know love is to know God.

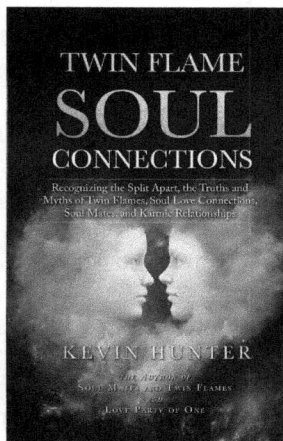

Twin Flame Soul Connections discusses and lists some of the various myths and truths surrounding the Twin Flames, and how to identify if you've come into contact with your Twin Flame, or if you know someone who has. The ultimate goal is not to find ones Twin Flame, but to awaken ones heart to love, and to work on becoming complete and whole as an individual soul through spiritual self-mastery, life lessons, growth, and raising your consciousness. Your soul's life was born out of love and will die right back into that love.

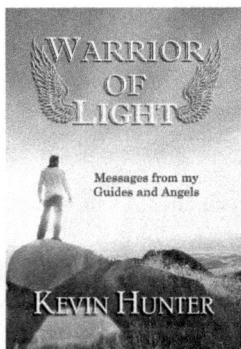

WARRIOR OF LIGHT
Messages from my Guides and Angels

There are legions of angels, spirit guides, and departed loved ones in heaven that watch and guide you on your journey here on Earth. They are around to make your life easier and less stressful. Learn how you can recognize the guidance of your own Spirit team of guides and angels around you. Author, Kevin Hunter, relays heavenly guided messages about getting humanity, the world, and yourself into shape. He delivers the guidance passed onto him by his own Spirit team on how to fine tune your body, soul and raise your vibration. Doing this can help you gain hope and faith in your own life in order to start attracting in more abundance.

EMPOWERING SPIRIT WISDOM
A Warrior of Light's Guide on Love, Career and the Spirit World

Kevin Hunter relays heavenly, guided messages for everyday life concerns with his book, *Empowering Spirit Wisdom*. Some of the topics covered are your soul, spirit and the power of the light, laws of attraction, finding meaningful work, transforming your professional and personal life, navigating through the various stages of dating and love relationships, as well as other practical affirmations and messages from the Archangels. Kevin Hunter passes on the sensible wisdom given to him by his own Spirit team in this inspirational book.

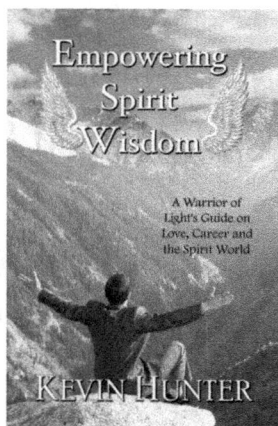

DARKNESS OF EGO

In *Darkness of Ego*, author Kevin Hunter infuses some of the guidance, messages, and wisdom he's received from his Spirit team surrounding all things ego related. The ego is one of the most damaging culprits in human life. Therefore, it is essential to understand the nature of the beast in order to navigate gracefully out of it when it spins out of control. Some of the topics covered in *Darkness of Ego* are humanity's destruction, mass hysteria, karmic debt, and the power of the mind, heaven's gate, the ego's war on love and relationships, and much more.

REACHING FOR THE WARRIOR WITHIN

Reaching for the Warrior Within is the author's personal story recounting a volatile childhood. This led him to a path of addictions, anxiety and overindulgence in alcohol, drugs, cigarettes and destructive relationships. As a survival mechanism, he split into many different "selves". He credits turning his life around, not by therapy, but by simultaneously paying attention to the messages he has been receiving from his Spirit team in Heaven since birth.

REALM OF THE WISE ONE

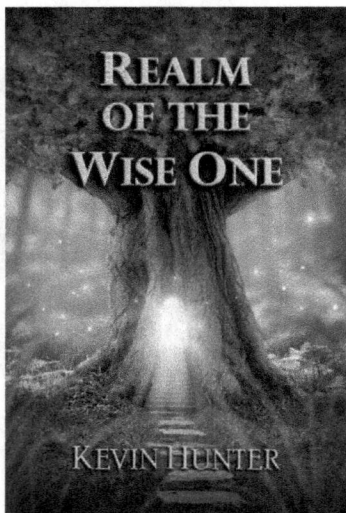

In the Spirit Worlds and the dimensions that exist, reside numerous kingdoms that house a plethora of Spirits that inhabit various forms. One of these tribes is called the Wise Ones, a darker breed in the spirit realm who often chooses to incarnate into a human body one lifetime after another for important purposes.

The *Realm of the Wise One* takes you on a magical journey to the spirit world where the Wise Ones dwell. This is followed with in-depth and detailed information on how to recognize a human soul who has incarnated from the Wise One Realm. Author, Kevin Hunter, is a Wise One who uses the knowledge passed onto him by his Spirit team of Guides and Angels to relay the wisdom surrounding all things Wise One. He discusses the traits, purposes, gifts, roles, and personalities among other things that make up someone who is a Wise One. Wise Ones have come in the guises of teachers, shaman, leaders, hunters, mediums, entertainers and others. *Realm of the Wise One* is an informational guide devoted to the tribe of the Wise Ones, both in human form and on the other side.

IGNITE YOUR INNER LIFE FORCE

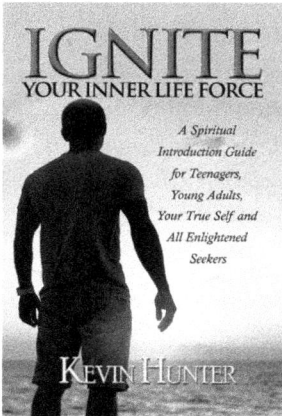

Ignite Your Inner Life Force is an introduction guide for teens, young adults, and anyone seeking answers, messages, and guidance and surrounding spiritual empowerment. This is from understanding what Heaven, the soul, and spiritual beings are to knowing when you are connecting with your Spirit team of Guides and Angels. Some of the topics covered are communicating with Heaven, working with your Spirit team, what your higher self is, your life purpose and soul contract, what the ego is, love and relationships, your vibration energy, shifting your consciousness and thinking for yourself even when you stand alone. This is an in-depth primer manual offering you foundation as you find a higher purpose navigating through your personal journey in today's modern day practical world.

AWAKEN YOUR CREATIVE SPIRIT

Your creative spirit is more than being artistic and getting involved in creativity pursuits, although this is a good part of it. When your creative spirit is activated by a high vibration state of being, then this is the space you create from. You can apply this to your dealings in life, your creative and artistic pursuits, and to having a greater communication line with your Spirit team on the Other Side. *Awaken Your Creative Spirit* is an overview of what it means to have access to Divine assistance and how that plays a part in arousing the muse within you in order to bring your state of mind into a happier space.

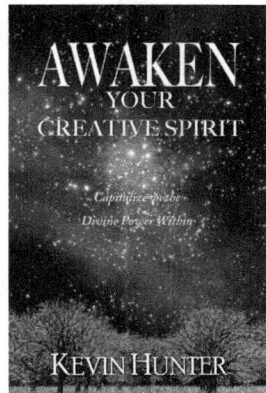

THE *WARRIOR OF LIGHT* SERIES OF POCKET BOOKS

Spirit Guides and Angels, Soul Mates and Twin Flames, Raising Your Vibration, Connecting with the Archangels, Twin Flame Soul Connections, Attracting in Abundance, Monsters and Angels, The Four Psychic Clair Senses, The Seven Deadly Sins, Love Party of One, Abundance Enlightenment, and *Divine Messages for Humanity*

METAPHYSICAL DIVINE WISDOM
BOOK SERIES

On Psychic Spirit Team Heaven Communication
On Soul Consciousness and Purpose
On Increasing Prayer with Faith for an Abundant Life
On Balancing the Mind, Body, and Soul
On Manifesting Fearless Assertive Confidence
On Universal, Physical, Spiritual and Soul Love

♥

About Kevin Hunter

Kevin Hunter is the metaphysical author of dozens of spiritually based books that include *Warrior of Light, Transcending Utopia, Stay Centered Psychic Warrior, Metaphysical Divine Wisdom Series, Empowering Spirit Wisdom, Realm of the Wise One, Reaching for the Warrior Within, Darkness of Ego, Living for the Weekend, Ignite Your Inner Life Force, Awaken Your Creative Spirit,* and *Tarot Card Meanings.*

His pocket books include, *Spirit Guides and Angels, Soul Mates and Twin Flames, Raising Your Vibration, Divine Messages for Humanity, Connecting with the Archangels, The Seven Deadly Sins, Four Psychic Clair Senses, Monsters and Angels, Twin Flame Soul Connections, Attracting in Abundance, Love Party of One* and *Abundance Enlightenment.* His non-spiritual related works include the horror drama, *Paint the Silence,* and the modern day love story, *Jagger's Revolution.*

Kevin started out in the entertainment business in 1996 as the personal development assistant guy to one of Hollywood's most respected acting talents, Michelle Pfeiffer, at her former boutique production company, Via Rosa Productions. She dissolved her company after several years and he made a move into coordinating film productions for the studios. His film credits include One Fine Day, A Thousand Acres, The Deep End of the Ocean, Crazy in Alabama, The Perfect Storm, Original Sin, Harry Potter & the Sorcerer's Stone, Dr. Dolittle 2, and Carolina. He considers himself a beach bum born and raised in Southern California. For more information and books visit: www.kevin-hunter.com

www.ingramcontent.com/pod-product-compliance
Lightning Source LLC
Chambersburg PA
CBHW060234050426
42448CB00009B/1438